Chair Shots and Other Obstacles

Bobby Heenan
with
Steve Anderson

Sports Publishing L.L.C.
www.sportspublishingllc.com

©2004 Bobby Heenan and Steve Anderson
  All rights reserved.

Director of production: Susan M. Moyer
Project manager: Jim Henehan
Dust jacket design: Joseph Brumleve
Developmental editor: Kipp Wilfong
Copy editor: Holly Birch
Photo editor: Erin Linden-Levy

Ilustrations by Steve Anderson

ISBN: 1-58261-762-7

Printed in the United States of America

Sports Publishing L.L.C.
www.sportspublishingllc.com

For Yennar, Eve Hedgecock,
Harold Anderson, and Andrew Graff

Table of Contents

Foreword

The first time I saw Bobby Heenan, I was wrestling for Verne Gagne at the Amphitheater in Chicago. It must have been my first or second week in the business and he was managing Blackjack Lanza and Blackjack Mulligan against Crusher and Bruiser. He was also causing a full-scale riot.

That day had such an impact on me. Bobby Heenan overall was so impacting that a match sometimes wasn't any good until he got active. As a fan, I would watch a match where he was managing and just couldn't wait for Bobby to get involved. He had so much energy. Bobby was a better worker than 90 percent of the guys he managed. In fact, he is one of the top 10 workers I've met in my life.

He still has an impact on me. The position I'm in now with WWE is very similar to what he did throughout his career. If I go out and manage one of my guys and I get involved in the match a lot, it kind of takes away from those guys in the ring. I'm in a no-win situation, but that's what the fans want. I learned from the best.

As a professional, Bobby taught me how important energy was and to always be focused on whatever you're doing. How you needed to keep moving, keep performing, and do the little things, like keeping your hair flopping around.

Bobby and his professionalism always impressed me. He carried himself well and dressed real sharp. I've known Bobby for 30 years now, and he is a tremendous guy, but he never showed the fans that side of him. In fact, I don't know what a fan could learn from Bobby, because he was always "Bobby Heenan" around the fans.

I think that if Bobby regrets treating the fans badly, he's wrong for saying that. It's a natural feeling after all he's been through, but the fans love that and it's what they expect. If I were Bobby Heenan, I'd want the fans to know that I hated them every time they bought a ticket. That's what made him good and a role model for others who followed in his footsteps. The fans hated Bobby as a manager, but loved him as a performer. They wanted to kill him when he was out there. Bobby carried himself like that, so arrogant. It's what he was paid to do, and he was the best at it. It doesn't mean that he wasn't a good guy, but he wasn't getting paid to be a good guy. He was being paid to make the fans mad.

He could make them laugh, too. I was on a plane once with Bobby when this girl walked up to him and asked him, "What do you do for a living?"

Bobby said, "I'm a salesman."

"What do you sell?"

"Backdrops and turnbuckles."

Bobby is such a well-rounded guy. He was wild like I'm wild. But I know that when he went home and took off that Superman cape, he was one hell of a father and husband. Most of us are family guys, but Bobby was very classy about it. He kept his family away from the business, which is very important. For some reason, and it happens in every phase in life, there were a lot of people in our business where class was something that was rare.

It's funny. We're in such an insensitive business, but we are such great friends at the same time. We knew to separate our personal lives from the road. I could be drunk with him one night and have a very serious conversation the next day. To this day, I'll talk to him on the holidays and all the important days in life. He'll call and ask how the family is doing.

But when I think about Bobby Heenan, I think about one of the greatest. He was a phenomenal performer and he was unselfish. He got beat up every night, got up, and did it again the next night. He was an example of working hard, and he added so much to every show he was on. I hope he gets his due, because I believe he was the best manager of all time, if not one of the best workers.

I tell the guys now, "You have no idea how good this guy was."

Bobby could do it all.

—Ric Flair

Introduction

The first thing I'd like to do is to inform anyone who is reading this, that I'm fairly confident that you either purchased the book, mooched it off somebody, or you're just a plain deadbeat. I'm kidding, of course. That's what "The Brain" in me would say. Keep in mind that sometimes Ray Heenan and Bobby "The Brain" Heenan overlap. When I was younger, I was a lot more like him than I am today. I was more mischievous. I would just do things to see if I could do them. I never did things out of anger, unlike "The Brain." I never get mad, because that's a weakness, but I do get even, like putting Quaker Oats in the radiator of your truck or limburger on your engine block. As I got older, my goal was primarily to entertain and, honestly, to still see if could do it.

I suppose you're wondering how a professional wrestler can write a self-help book. Bottom line: I've got common sense about many things. Of course, we probably all think we do. We all think that we are smarter than we are. I don't pretend to be something I'm not. Never have. Never will. The advice I give is based on my experiences and observations. You can take some and leave some, which is what you should do with all advice.

I come to this with a background of being a wrestler and a manager, even though I didn't really wrestle and didn't really manage. I'll get into that later in the book. It was just a title for me. A lot of people take jobs because they just want the title, but they can't perform the basic responsibilities, this happens both in wrestling and in life. Then again, a lot of people are qualified for the jobs, but they can't kiss ass, which seems to be a requirement in professional wrestling, and I'm sure many other industries as well.

I do want to thank you for taking the time to read my words and those of my good friend, author, and cartoonist, Steve Anderson. I think it will be a lot of fun, which is the point. I don't take myself too seriously, and neither should you. There will be wrestling in it for the fans. There's going to be life in it for people curious to see what a retired wrestler/manager/broadcaster has to say. Sometimes wrestling and life experiences overlapped as well. There are lessons I learned in wrestling that can apply to anyone's life. I'll talk about what things I think people need to know. And other things that people don't need to know. So, mind your business, humanoids. It's going to be interesting. I will show you how to face the "The Brains" in this world and when and when not to act like one.

Speaking of "The Brain," keep a look out for his influence throughout the entire book.

I have a confession to make.
Yes, I bet on wrestling.
I'm sorry.

—Bobby Heenan

CHAPTER 1

So, You Want To Get Into Professional Wrestling

One time I was traveling with Gorilla Monsoon to Toronto. He was so tired. They had us in so many towns, and on top of everything else, he had just had his little toe amputated because of his diabetes. There I was, pushing a 350-pound guy named "Gorilla" in a wheelchair through the airport, just like I did in those big chairs in Atlantic City on Prime Time Wrestling. There was a line for handicapped people, so I went in that line for him.

"What is your citizenship?" the guy at the counter asked.

"United States," we both said.

"What is it that you do?"

A tired Monsoon yelled, "They fire us out of the cannon until they kill us! We're circus people!"

People always come up to me and ask me, "How can I get into professional wrestling?" If I were honest, my response to them would be, "What's the matter? Aren't they hiring any more drug dealers or bank robbers? You could do all that and really have a good time. Why would you want to get into this? Do something legitimate."

"A friend in need is a pest."

In all seriousness, I don't know why anyone would get into wrestling except for the glory. Don't get me wrong. This business has been very good to me. I have raised a family and buried my mother from the money I made off professional wrestling. I'm not bitter and I've seen the world and made lifelong friendships. For me, it was a dream come true and more. But with every dream you have, reality comes in and wakes you up. I'll get into that later, but, for now, let me deal with this question that I hear so often.

Bottom line. If you're getting into professional wrestling for anything but the money, you're a fool. Yes, you can be dedicated. Yes, you can be for the fans. But make no mistake about it. It's a business. First of all, you can get hurt real bad, and if that happens, you're of no use to a promoter. I've had both ankles sprained, my collarbone and neck broken, and operations on my knee and elbow. I even developed a cyst on my side from all the bumps I took—a cyst that got infected following my radiation and chemotherapy treatments after my cancer surgery.

If you get hurt, there's no hospitalization provided by the promotion. I broke my neck in 1983 and I couldn't afford to have it operated on. It wasn't until 1995, after I left WWF and went to work for Turner Broadcasting and WCW, that I was no longer considered a wrestler or manager or even considered talent. I was an announcer and a full-time employee. That's the exception to the rule, but that's how I got my insurance and how I could pay for my neck and cancer operations. If I had to cover those expenses, I would have been in deep water. Anyone would. Whether I had the money or not is not the issue. Plus, with my wife getting cancer after me, that would have been $300,000 to $500,000 with everything we went through. That can knock you out pretty quick, whether you have the money or not. If you don't have it, you don't know where to get it. If you have it, you won't have it for long and it's gone.

If a guy is hurt nowadays, a promotion like WWE will pay him for a while and maybe even pay him the whole time. I'm not sure, I never had that luxury. After my neck operation in 1995, I never missed a day of work. I was in the operating room for seven hours, came home, and then went to Atlanta with a neck brace on to do voiceovers. The doctors told me not to fly, because you never know when you're going to get turbulence. I had to wear the brace the whole time. Plus, it's hard to drink on a plane with the neck brace on. The olives keep getting caught in your throat.

And the treatment doesn't change, no matter where you are on the card, whether you're in the main event or the opening match. I remember one night where Lou Thesz broke his leg while wrestling. The next night, in St. Louis, he taped up his ankle and wrestled one hour with

Dick the Bruiser. Sure, he was dedicated to the business. And he was the world's champion at the time in the main event. But he probably needed and wanted the money and would not have received it if he took the night off.

There are no benefits in wrestling for the guys, and there should be something for them. There should be retirement after so many years. A gold watch or a "gold potato" for all the stiff shots we took in the ring. Professional wrestling is the only business like it in the world.

In today's wrestling world, guys like Hulk Hogan could afford to get hurt and take time off to recover, but if you're the guy in the first match trying to catch a break, you may not be able to.

Even if you were able to work, you weren't guaranteed a payoff. Sometimes you'd wrestle on TV, and if you went over, you got nothing. The guy who did the job made 10 bucks. Why? Well, you went over, but you're also doing the house show. You have more exposure and you'll make more money at the house show and down the line more so than the guy you beat and who just got paid more than you did.

I got merchandise money from the WWF but never really knew how much a Bobby Heenan action figure sold. I know it sold well, because the Hulk Hogan doll needed someone to wrestle. It's "First Count" in action, just like when we got our payoffs. They count the tickets and count the money, long before we ever see anything.

The promoters don't pay for your hotel rooms. They don't pay for your rental cars. They cover your transportation, but you have to take the cheapest flight they can find for you. That doesn't seem so bad, but if you're a big guy like Earthquake or the Big Bossman and get stuck in 32F, the middle seat, it's hard to fly three or four hours like that and then have to think about flying back. Then you have to stand in line for a half hour for your rental car and wait another half hour for the bus. You get to the hotel and there is no guarantee that the room will even be ready. Then you have to get to the building. Hell, first you have to *find* the building. Then, you return the car at 6 a.m. the next day, only to find out that they haven't opened yet. It was more fun in the '60s when we were driving around in cars with four guys. Just good friends laughing.

On top of the hectic travel, there are such high expectations of what wrestlers should be doing in the ring. That comes from promoters, and it comes from fans too. You can only inflict so much damage to your body. Back in the '60s, promoters liked you to take bumps and give blood—"getting juice or color" means cutting yourself for you moochers who don't know about wrestling, didn't buy the first book, or are bumming this book off someone.

Professional wrestling was natural for me. I always had the ability to bump and bleed. Come to think of it, I wouldn't have been a bad "hit and run" victim.

Now, promoters want you to really look like you're in top shape and fly around that ring. If you don't have what they see as good matches, the promotion simply doesn't want to use you. That shatters a lot of dreams for good wrestlers. But there are a lot of people in the business who think that they're a lot better than they are.

Today's style is different from what it was just a few years ago. I could get in the ring right now with Paul Orndorff, who is retired, and get heat. I would do an interview about what I think of him and he does one on what he thinks of me.

We could stand there in the ring. When the bell rings and we look at each other, I'd back off in the corner and we'd walk around. Finally, we would lock up. Then, I'd pull a cheap shot on him and jump out. I'd argue with a fan or tell the referee to check him for a foreign object. I could stall and take time until the people would be so upset that they would want to see Orndorff come get me. We could tear the place down today and really get fans riled. I could do it by just pulling his hair and then telling the referee I didn't.

That is, if the referee didn't see it.

Everybody does everything in front of the referee nowadays. All the heat goes on the ref and, with all due respect, no one bought a ticket to see the "Earl Hebners" of this world. Everybody pulls hair, hits each other with chairs, and there are no count-outs or disqualifications for it. But if I snuck something or pulled hair and then the ref asked me if I did that, I'd shake my head wildly and make my hair go all over for all to see and yell, "No!" as loud as I could.

The place would go nuts for Orndorff and me, and we wouldn't have to go through a single table. That's called working.

You have to do minimal things to be a heel. Honestly, you get more heat when you sneak. I snuck out of the house four times last year and boy did I get heat. All a heel has to do is be a sneaky little coward and take bumps. That's it. You don't have to do anything else. Wrestlers and fans forget that you don't have to be strong to be in our business, you just have to look strong. You don't have to be tough, but you sure as hell have to sound tough. You want to be humble? Be a babyface and make the people cry. I'd rather be a heel and scare the hell out of them or piss them off.

Now, they're doing routines, and I think it's ridiculous because it is just so much effort and it means so little. These young wrestlers are flying around the ring and they are inevitably going to get hurt. The "no insurance" card is played again. Oh sure, a promoter such as Vince McMahon may take care of you for a little bit, but if you break your back, he is not going to take care of you for the rest of your life. It doesn't make Vince a bad man, just a business man.

If anyone is reading this thinking that they want to be a wrestler and nothing will ever stop them, then God bless you. Be a wrestler. I felt that way. It was something deep inside of me, and no one, no matter who it was, could have talked me out of it. But once you start going through five tables or fall off a steel cage onto a floor, it will be called a truly spectacular moment by the announcers, the fans, and the people who cover professional wrestling. But once it's done, it's history. Now, it's up to the next guy to go through six tables or dive off a higher cage. Who knows what they are going to want to do next and who knows where it will stop?

So, these unbelievable bumps are being taken, and guess what? No one sells them, so those moves end up not meaning anything. Like I said, it's all routines, just like the Rockettes. If you jump off the rope, chances are you're not going to get hurt. But if you jump off a cage, you will get hurt and that's the problem. The standard has been set, and it may be just another reason to stay far away from professional wrestling.

Believe me if you believe nothing else, the promotion does not care about you. You're a product to be marketed. If you can get through your wrestling life without a career-ending injury, that doesn't matter. You are finished when a promoter says you're finished. That is just the way it is. Take all the silly bumps you want to and the promoters will tell you the goofier, the better, because it makes their shows memorable and spectacular. People will want to come to the next show or buy the DVD. But when you are hurt, you are hurt, and it's over. The physical pain may or may not go away, but the emotional pain will stay with you forever.

Working the wrestling style I described is the way they learned. I'm not saying today's way is wrong, just different. But I still say I could go out there and have any type of match and be entertaining. No chairs. No tables. No ladders.

I don't know how anyone would get a start in professional wrestling these days. WWE uses Ohio Valley Wrestling as a developmental territory and wrestling school. I don't know if the wrestlers have to pay for it or even if the wrestlers are guaranteed anything. It's just very hard to get into the business and make a full-time living. The hardest thing after getting into the business is just being able to stay in the business. You can stay in the business as long as you want and I know guys who say that they've been "in the business" 10 years, but only had three matches.

At the time I got into wrestling, I really didn't plan to do so, and it wasn't by choice. I was drafted. I was working as a car jockey at a Ford Dealer in Indianapolis, bringing the cars up from the lot to the mechanics. They would get them ready. I would basically sit and hold a washrag all day, smoke cigarettes with a guy named Willie, and listen to the Four Tops. That's all I did. I loved it. It was the best job I ever had. I loved wrestling and loved being a part of it, but never did I ask to be wrestler or a manager.

At the time I broke in, I was working for Championship Wrestling promoted by Dick the Bruiser and Wilbur Snyder. I was selling Cokes and carrying jackets. They had a manager named Captain Willie, who was a goof, and Bruiser didn't like him, so he got fired. I wasn't begging to get into the business, but Dick needed a manager for the Assassins. I was drafted and became a manager without asking anyone if I could give it a try.

And you probably wonder what kept me in it for all those years. Honestly, I was lazy. I didn't want to get up in the morning and be a milkman, work in a spring factory, or put up hockey boards in the Coliseum for the rest of my life. I didn't want to go back to a hardware store or the Ford dealership. I saw Willie break-dance as much as I could possibly tolerate. Professional wrestling provided me a good job for the money, and it was exciting. There were a lot of women there. I felt like somebody. I had bleached blond hair and wore nice clothes.

Laziness kept me motivated, but the biggest motivation of all was feeding my mother and my grandmother. Plus, I love to be a ham, and I love to entertain.

The business is work—which means it's not real, for you people who are mooching the book. Wrestling is roller derby without shoes. It sounds funny coming from me, but I always resented wrestling being called a sport. It's not a sport. It's a predetermined event. Some bitched about the coverage we did and didn't get, but I can understand why sportswriters never wrote about wrestling on the sports page or sports broadcasters would never cover it. For us to say it is a sport, well, we just look like idiots.

Think about it. There are no masked men in the on-deck circle at Yankee Stadium. They don't announce a guy starting for the Lakers from Parts Unknown. How can I work for a promoter and not tell him who I am? How do I get paid? Only in professional wrestling could there be a guy from Borneo who supposedly spoke absolutely no English, but wore a UCLA ring while he wrestled. George "The Animal" Steele supposedly could only say "Hey you" and "Mine," yet he wore a Michigan State watch and a ring from the wrestling team.

Have you ever gotten into a fight and airplane spin a guy or ass bump a guy on the bar? The average fight lasts 30 seconds. Professional wrestlers can compete in a one-hour Broadway show and they don't have a bruise on them, and they got hit by chairs, too. When I was a kid, I threw a wrought-iron kitchen chair at my grandmother. Wrought-iron bounces. It hit the wall, bounced back, and hit me right between the eyes. I looked like a raccoon for a month. That took four seconds. Three seconds for me to grab and throw the chair and one second for it to clock me. Hell, a mosquito lands on your arm and bites you, you can see it for a month.

I felt stupid, and I could never defend it to people. That always got me. Honestly, I was always embarrassed to be a wrestler because I had to protect what I did. The promoters would brainwash you, telling you not to talk to people about the business. We were told, at all costs, to not smarten anyone up. But was that the only way to save the business, or was it the only way to save the promoters' own companies and meal tickets?

I know there are a lot of people at home watching wrestling on television, knowing it's a work and thinking to themselves, "I could do that. I could be an actor." Believe me, acting is a very hard business. Not only do you have to know your lines, but you have to know *their* lines. As much as I did comedy in wrestling over 40 years and got my share of laughs, I never said anything scripted. The closest I came to using a script was when I did the movie *Time Masters* with Gene Okerlund.

To do a whole show or movie with a lot of dialogue is tough. Some actors are taught to learn their lines from singing instructors who teach them rhythmically. Acting is not a part-time job. You can't take a couple of months and become an actor. Those people are out there working constantly. They're out there doing jobs as waiters or busboys to pay the bills. Many are unemployed, but they continue to go to casting calls every day, just waiting to get their break.

I think people would have respected us more if we admitted that we were great athletic actors, not professional wrestlers. Robin Williams is a great comedic actor. Sir Lawrence Olivier was a great Shakespearean and dramatic actor. Hulk Hogan is a great athletic actor, but he'll never win the Oscar. Mickey Rooney was a great actor, but he couldn't play the Scorpion King. He'd need a boost to get on the horse.

To tell the fans that professional wrestling is real is an insult to them. They all know it's not real. It's just a different form of entertainment—sports entertainment. But for being actors, we received not one residual because we're considered a sport like basketball and hockey. We're not.

We should get the same type of residuals like *Cheers* or *Friends*. They're pre-determined shows, just like *Raw*, *Nitro*, and *Smackdown*.

When it comes to professional wrestling, I know nothing else like it, except prostitution. Promoters are pimps in good-looking suits, and the wrestlers are the whores. There are a lot of similarities if you think about it. Wrestlers wear shiny and glittery costumes. Someone tells them what to do. Pimps want a prostitute to bounce on the bed and promoters want wrestlers to bounce on the mat. Both "encounters" are booked beforehand, with one person telling the other what they will and won't do. And they tell you you're great when you may not have been. If you're bad at it, they stop using you. Take a week off and don't get paid. They tell you how much time they want you for and who you're working with and how much you make. And you travel around.

It's the same thing.

Promoters and pimps don't really yell, because they know if they yelled too much, that person might quit and the promoter or pimp would make less money. But, in the end, there's always another guy waiting in the wings. I was one of those who could have been easily replaced by my promoter/pimp. Just call me Trixie.

Think of it this way. Imagine applying for a job in professional wrestling just like you would any other part-time or full-time job, say in the United States Postal Service. This is how the interview would go if the post office was like a professional wrestling promotion.

"What days do I have off?" you'd ask.

The boss would chuckle, "It beats me."

"Will I get paid vacation or summers off?"

"I don't think so."

"Will I work eight hours a day?"

"You could. I'm not sure. You could work 14."

"All I have to do is deliver the mail?"

"No, you may have to grease the trucks or even mop the floor if the janitor doesn't show up," the boss would say.

"Well, what would I make?"

"How do I know?"

"Is there any insurance?"

"Are you kidding?"

Give me that job. Where can I sign up? I did it. We all did it. And now they want me to write a book on giving advice?

What did I do for 40 years? I carried a razor blade in my pocket. I bleached my hair. I changed my name and I said I was from Beverly Hills. I was on an airplane one day and the guy sitting next to me asked me where I was from. I told him Beverly Hills. "Just my luck," he said,

"So am I. What part of Beverly Hills do you live in?" I didn't know any street names. I only knew the zip code because I saw that "90210" show. If anyone had asked me the zip code before that show was on, I would have never known.

Frankly, I would suggest not getting into wrestling. I would suggest getting an education. If you're not good scholastically, get a vocation. Learn how to do something with your hands. Learn how to repair cars. Learn a trade or something creative.

That's not to say that wrestlers are not educated people. While a lot of the guys have little if any formal training for anything but wrestling, a great many of them attended and graduated college, such as Nick Bockwinkel, Tito Santana, Baron Von Raschke.

Just know that you're not going to get anything out of professional wrestling when you're done. There's no pension. While you're in it, promotion and elevation are hard to come by. There's little opportunity in the way of commercial endorsements and, if there is, it's usually not a mainstream product. I wouldn't even suggest backyard wrestling as a way in, because they simply don't know what they're doing. It's like a kid driving a car at 14, pretending he's a race car driver. It's just as dangerous.

Enjoy wrestling for the entertainment value—or not. If you don't watch wrestling, turn it off. Some people don't like certain sports or types of entertainment. I don't watch hockey because it's too violent to me and I'm not a violent person. I know what you're thinking. He's a wrestler, but he's not violent? No, I'm an actor, and I don't like to see people get hit from behind. Plus I can't read the names of the players on a hockey team. It's like looking at eye charts.

If you want to get into something, try the medical industry. Perform plastic surgery, for example, and specialize in breast enhancements. You get to see women from the waist up nude and they pay you for it. You get to look at them and touch them, when you're done and before. Come to think of it, maybe I need to go to medical school, but it will take me until I'm 78 to put my shingle out there. Shouldn't be too hard. Finish the eighth grade, get my high school diploma, and go to college.

But I won't be a proctologist. Who would want to be a proctologist? No one ever comes to the office with a healthy ass. It's always a sick ass. You're always working with assholes.

It's like the doctor who came in the examining room with a thermometer behind his ear. The patient asked, "What's that?"

"Oh my God," the doctor said. "Some asshole has my pencil."

If you're pursuing a dream, think about the reality of it. Think about the future of it. If you're athletically inclined, professional football and many other sports provide pensions. You have to consider that.

If you want an eight-hour day, look somewhere else. You leave the house at 10:00 in the morning to make a noon flight. If it's a two-hour flight, between getting off the plane, getting your rental car, and driving to your hotel, you're not at your hotel until 4:00. Then you have to leave for the building at 5:00—hoping you can find it by 6:00. Then you go on at 9:45. You're out of the building and get back to your hotel by 11:30 or midnight. That's 14 hours right there.

Plus, you're away from home all the time. I never liked that part of it. I'm a home guy. I love my home. I like to be at home with my family and friends more than I ever loved the wrestling business. But I could never make any money at home with my friends. They're deadbeats.

In a wrestling locker room, it was much different. If anyone from the outside came into our dressing room, we wouldn't talk to them simply because they didn't belong there. We were hiding something. It was a whole different world that others would have never believed.

But that doesn't mean there was always a strong union, brotherhood, or fellowship that existed with the guys. If you were in the bar and if a guy got into a fight, everyone wanted to help him. It was like an unwritten law. But once we walked into that dressing room, everyone wanted everyone else's spot. It all came down to that payoff.

I think there is a brotherhood in wrestling to a degree, but not as much as you might think. I have close friends who are probably the only guys no one has ever said anything bad about: Ray Stevens, Baron Von Raschke, and Red Bastien. People may have said bad things about me and others—and maybe deservedly so—but nothing has ever been said bad about those men. Sadly, there are guys in this business who didn't want to see Baron, Ray, or Red draw money in the main event because they wanted that shot. The special relationships I had with all my friends are very few and far between.

I've had some great relationships in this business. There are so many people on top of the three I just mentioned. I could just go on and on, and if they're not mentioned in the book, I'm really sorry. I should mention all of them, and I do care about them. I do know a lot of people. For example, John Tolos called me while I was sick. He had never called me in his life. We were in Minneapolis together in the AWA and only get to see each other at the annual Cauliflower Alley banquet. He just called to say "Hi." We may never talk again for a year or ever. But he's an example of a good friend. Sadly, a rare example.

People lead very busy lives, and it's hard to keep in touch. You may not hear from someone as much as you would want to, but that doesn't mean that they're not a friend.

It was just hard in wrestling to even get close to other people if you wanted to. You're only in a territory for six months or a year. Sometimes their wives didn't like each other. Other times it was jealousy toward the guy in the ring about stealing a gimmick, getting a push, or never being willing to drive to the towns. It's always something that prevents friendships from forming.

Many times, it was the promotion or just the overall environment that promoters created. We never knew what we were going to make money-wise, because everything was on a shoestring budget. Everybody was worried about their job. The promotion could fire you at any time, but if you wanted to leave, you had to give a six-week notice. And, if you did leave, your old boss would call your new boss you were going to work for and say that you're not reliable and can't be trusted. When you showed up in that promotion, they would use you, but you wouldn't become their champion, because they would be scared that you could pull up stakes and go. So, you had to kiss their ass, stay the six weeks, say nothing, and take what they give you before you leave.

Working relationships were very hard and they rarely turned into personal relationships or friendships. One guy had "First Count." One guy paid you and hired and fired you. They wouldn't tell you how much the house drew and even if they did tell you, you didn't believe them. Hell, we never knew how much money we were going to make. I would walk up to a promoter and say, "Hey, we sold out tonight," only to have him say, "Well, it's like this. We gave an entire section of tickets to war veterans." That creates strained relationships, but that's how the business is. But no matter what, a lot of guys continued to brown nose and suck up to the promoter, but that doesn't always help.

There's no "I" in "team" and there's definitely little team effort in professional wrestling. For instance, on the Cubs you have 25 guys on a team. I guarantee you that someone wants Sammy Sosa to pull a hamstring so he can get his spot. He wants to take over for Sosa, so he can get that job and make his money. They're all on the team bus together, and they all want to win that game. Just like all the wrestlers want the show to go well and the house to make money. But in the end, they all want to be that one guy who hits the ninth-inning home run with the bases loaded to come from behind and win. I don't think anyone wants to see anyone else hurt, but if someone pulls a hammy, they pull a hammy. Somebody always wants your job if you're doing better than they are.

It's weird. Maybe professional wrestling is like Hollywood too, in that respect. When an actor is sick or dying, everyone comes to help. But when it comes to getting a part, they want that same person to fail.

But in spite of that, professional wrestlers were a lot closer in the old days, because they spent more time in cars together. In many ways, the "older" wrestlers were still great examples for me, because they took everything in stride—their payoffs, bumps, and their love lives. I never remember a wrestler coming in to a locker room, throwing down his gym bag and screaming, "Damn, I don't know how I'm going to pay the mortgage. My wife is fooling around with another guy. My kids are flunking school. My car is going to get repossessed." We all tried to keep things light in the dressing room, nice and relaxed. Those were the best of times in those locker rooms. Not the travel. Not waiting in line for an hour to get a ticket or a rental car. Or figuring out where the hotel and building were.

Plus, if you get a great guy in the ring, that can be relaxing as well. You were at home, and you felt that was your domain, just like that locker room. That's why very few outside of the business were let in there. I'm friends with a lot of baseball people, and that locker room environment is completely different. Jimmy Bank, a good friend of mine who is the press secretary for the Chicago Cubs, takes care of me every time I get to Chicago. He took me to the locker room once and introduced me to Sammy Sosa, who autographed a baseball for my son-in-law, John. We were just talking, and everyone was very nice. I was more than welcome, even though I was not in the baseball business.

You can always tell a wrestler is good if he draws money and gets heat. An average fan can go out to a show, watch a wrestler, and then tell after one match if they like him or not. There are some guys who get better. There are some guys who are the shits in the beginning and never get better. They never made it. They're like a fart in a spacesuit.

But success in wrestling comes down to the booker liking you, not necessarily the promoter. If I was a promoter and I hired the booker, I'd tell him, "You run it. Don't bother me." But maybe my ideas aren't like his. I bring in two guys who I like, and they're not really that talented, but I like them. I will push them down everyone's throat until people buy tickets or not at all. Some bookers like to do that, because they like the guys and want to make them money. but if you really want to make everyone money, push a guy you don't like who can make you money and send a check to the other guy you like but who is the shits just to stay home.

The booker used to get a very small percentage. I was offered a job as a booker in a territory for $100 a week. He told me that whatever I booked myself into, such as the main event, I would make more. It was the same as working in the ring. But I'd have to be in the office five days a week, from 10:00 until 6:00 on the phone with the guys, kissing ass and lying. For a hundred bucks a week? No. But everyone wants to be a booker. It's about power and controlling things. Some bookers were good. Some were ridiculous, foolish, couldn't book anything, or even call a cab because they weren't in the business.

It's just like WCW where they put championships on non-wrestlers such as Buff Bagwell's mother and David Arquette. It was booked by people who had never been in the business. It sounds like I'm knocking them, but that's the truth. I couldn't run a hockey team or anything. I've only done one thing in my life and that's wrestling, make people laugh, and be stupid. I made a living off that.

You want to get into wrestling? Buy a ticket.

CHAPTER 2

Living a Dream

I remember the first time I saw my name on the marquee outside of the Indiana State Fair: "Bruiser and Crusher versus The Devil's Duo managed by Bobby Heenan." I had worked in that building before, but not as a wrestler, just a regular employee. I lived five blocks down the street from there. That was exciting.

As I said in my other book—not that any of you deadbeats who mooched this book know—when I was a kid watching wrestling at Marigold Wrestling in Chicago, I was mesmerized by the heel—or bad guy—and how he could control the crowd. I was amazed by how they could have such an influence on the fans. It would be just like someone seeing Frank Sinatra, Elvis Presley, or the Rolling Stones. They knew how to captivate a crowd. Many people dream about being famous as a rock star or movie star.

Everybody has a dream. Some people dream about being a movie star and actor. Others dream about becoming a boxer, basketball player, or wrestler. Still others have goals of being a banker or doctor. Some just want to be at home with their families in the house with the white picket fence and the kids and dog playing in the yard. All that stuff.

My grandfather, Adam J. Trembacz, owned a clothing store on the west side of Chicago. While I never asked him and really never knew, I'm sure that owning his own business was as close to achieving a dream as

"Remember that old saying, 'What the hell, use the bell.'"

he could imagine. He used to sell clothes to and rub shoulders with Al Capone and his gang. They used to come into his store and give my mother a dollar to watch the store while they did business. Keep in mind that a dollar was a lot of money back in the '20s. They'd go into a back room, take their guns off, and my grandfather would measure them for clothes.

You would think that having a relationship with Capone would be dangerous, but it actually paid off. One day, my grandfather's store was robbed. Burglars broke in and took everything. The first thing he did was to call Capone and tell him what happened. Capone said, "I'll get back to you." He called back two days later and told my grandfather, "You'll find all your clothes in the basement of the Longdale Avenue Police Station." The police had knocked over his store. It was a hard lesson for him. Who could he trust? Capone was a gangster who killed many people and broke a ton of other laws. He was a no-good mobster and criminal. "The Brain" would think he was one hell of a guy. Yet, the police—the people sworn to protect him—had committed the crime with Capone investigating and finding out what happened.

Sometimes I think he lived that dream of owning a store and working hard to stay away from my grandmother, who resembled Schultz on Hogan's Heroes. He was Polish and she was German. They had three children, and I don't have any idea how that happened. My mother told me that after the first child, she stayed in bed for a year while my grandfather went to Cuba all the time on "golfing trips." Yeah, right. He probably spent the weekend on Rush Street in Chicago.

He was like the mayor of the West Side of Chicago. In churches where people would hang up their hats, there are plaques that say "Courtesy of Adam J. Trembacz." He was a very important person in the neighborhood. Hell, he put his hands on Capone and even saw him in his shorts without getting shot or being fitted for cement shoes.

He died in 1929 after falling and breaking his kneecap. He tried to get up on his own, but he fell again. He eventually contracted gangrene and pneumonia.

I don't know what my mother's dream was, but I would hope that by supporting her, I helped her to live her life the way she wanted. I guess that's everyone's dream. Live life and be happy.

I knew some wrestlers who had dreams. Ric Flair had a dream. He wanted to become a wrestler. Andre the Giant realized at an early age that the Kentucky Derby was out for him. He was never going to ride Secretariat. He played soccer early on in his life, but found out that entertainment in wrestling and even movies was a great life for him.

For me, my dream of being in wrestling started when I was a kid. At first, I was just hooked on television. I would have trouble getting up in the morning and going to school, because I would stay up late watching television. It wasn't even on all night in the '50s, and I don't think we even got a television until around 1954. Broadcasts normally stopped at 11:00, but when I was 10 years old, I would stay up all night and just watch the test patterns. I thought it was a show about Indians. I could just stay up all night and listen to the old television hum. I could even sing along to "Sermonette," and I wasn't even religious. I just loved TV.

In the morning, forget it, I just couldn't get my ass out of bed. And when I did, instead of going to school, I'd want to stay home and watch TV. I was hooked, pure and simple. And then when wrestling was on TV, that's when I really enjoyed myself. It sure beat the Indian show and "Sermonette."

So as you can see, it was natural for me to become a wrestler. I was able to work nights and didn't have to worry about getting up in the morning. I only had to work 10 minutes. It was just the fun of entertaining. I'm a ham. It came so natural to me. When I was a kid, I used to get up and dance on the furniture while my mother would be watching Fred Astaire movies on television. I would jump up on the furniture and show off. Trust me, I still have the belt marks on my ass from my mother to show it.

I just lived day to day in the early part of my pro wrestling career. I never thought about it leading to where it is today, not to mention it becoming a full-time job where I would make a very good living. I was having fun and making five bucks a night. I had another job at the Ford dealership, so this was extra cash I could use for myself and to support my family. I was driving in a car all over the country with people I idolized when I was that punk television addict. I was drinking beer and meeting women. I didn't know where it was going. I had absolutely no idea. It was just fun.

It was so exciting. I was working in Indianapolis, my home at the time. I was traveling to Louisville (110 miles), Chicago (200 miles), Canada (300 miles), Terre Haute (75 miles), Muncie (25 miles), and Fort Wayne (150 miles). The biggest trip was 200 miles, and I was making more money than I was at the dealership. Not a whole lot more, but I was maybe making five to 20 dollars a night and I didn't have to work each and every day. All in all, I was probably making $80 to $100 a week.

The '60s were an eye-opener, because of the pure excitement. The only thing that came close to that for me was the '80s, when Vince McMahon charged full steam ahead and brought wrestling into the mainstream, making it what it should have been all along: entertainment. It was so much fun and we were finally getting respect. Before *Rock and Wrestling*, the big newspapers would never cover us, and the media treated us like carnies.

I never was world champion, because I didn't have the body for it. I realized that and was fine with it. It didn't shatter my dreams in the least. I knew I needed bigger arms and bigger legs, but I didn't like to work out. Like I said, I'm lazy. I don't like to do a whole lot of things.

I ended up doing just about everything in professional wrestling except promote. I did have 10 percent of an Indianapolis-based promotion for a brief time with Verne Gagne, but it never left the ground, so we didn't make any money. It wasn't anyone's fault. We just didn't have good TV. Also, I never wrestled a woman. But I have wrestled guys I wasn't too sure about.

Looking back at the good and bad of professional wrestling, I never really wanted to do anything else. It paid me the best for what I had the ability to do. It's all I had. I probably could and should have made more money, but I don't think I could have had any more fun doing anything else with all the people I've met, all the places I have been to, and all the things that I have seen.

When I was a kid, watching everything I could possibly watch, including cartoons, I never imagined that I would be a cartoon character myself. The WWF was getting so popular in the mid-80s, that a Saturday morning cartoon show was created with animated WWF wrestlers. It was called *Hulk Hogan's Rock and Wrestling*.

I was animated into a couple of episodes, but I mainly appeared in live vignettes that they showed before and after the cartoons. We taped it out in Los Angeles. Gene Okerlund and I did this bit where we pretended to be at my home in Beverly Hills when it was actually some luxury apartments. Gene—in his full tuxedo with the shoes, cufflinks, bowtie, and everything—and I were sitting by the pool when the phone rang. We both reached for it, but I "accidentally" bumped Gene and he fell into the pool. I picked up the phone, started talking, and completely ignored him.

After that, we both were done for the day. Gene immediately got out of the pool and we drove back to the hotel in a limousine.

We were standing in the elevator in the hotel and there was Gene wearing this completely soaked suit. It was like he put his clothes on before he got in the shower. Water was squishing and dripping all over. There were about seven people in the elevator who couldn't figure out what was going on. I looked over at him and said, "It's a little hot here."

"It's mostly humid," Gene said without missing a beat.

We taped another vignette where Gene was trying to get his money back from a vending machine that took it, but he couldn't get it to work. He called me over, and "The Brain" worked his magic on it, and all the money came out.

"Thank you," he said.

I said, "Well, if I'm 'The Brain' and you're not, I keep the money," and I left.

When I got home to Tampa after shooting that, they called me back and said I needed to go back out to L.A. and re-shoot it.

"Why?" I asked.

"What you did was stealing," I was told.

"So what you mean is you can't show stealing, but you can take dynamite and have the Road Runner pound it up the Coyote's ass all the way past his lung and blow him up?"

"Well that's animation. You're a live human being," this guy said.

So, I went back out there. It was very expensive because the studio flew us out first class each way and put us in the Universal Hotel. We ended up re-shooting the scene with Gene getting the money after all.

And it never aired.

Not only was it a waste of time and money, it was a dumb idea to make us go back out there. I think kids for the most part know the difference between right and wrong. Some do right. Some do wrong. But to say that a comedy character like "The Brain" would set an example for kids to steal money is stupid. I would like to think kids are smarter than that.

So, if there are any kids reading this—then again, you probably didn't pay for it or your old man is mooching it from someone—don't take money from other people, but if you see a Road Runner, I've got a few ideas.

First-class accommodations were the glamorous side of professional wrestling, especially when I was in the WWF. That was the dream come true. I flew on the MGM Grand plane. It was usually rented out to professional sports teams, but we were able to use it when flying to do work for the cartoon. MGM would send a car for us and pick us up at the hotel. We didn't have to worry about dealing with security at the airport because they let us go right through. The plane itself was a huge Lear jet. They prepared meals and baked cookies right on the plane. I sat on these swivel-around chairs, took advantage of the full bar, and read any kind of paper from any kind of city. It was full-blown luxury. Hell, it beat the plane they had in the AWA. It was a nice switch from that plane and others. I've flown on airlines that were so cheap, by the time the nuts got back to me, the sack was empty.

Everything in the WWF was first class, with limos and the accommodations. And, as usual, the boys would abuse things. They would order the limo driver to drive them to the gym or to a restaurant and force the driver to wait. On top of that, they would never tip the guy.

But if there was one dream that I was able to live more than anything, it was working with Gorilla Monsoon on Prime Time Wrestling. It was the most fun I ever had, bar none. On top of that, he was my best friend. How many people can say that they achieved a personal and professional dream at the same time, working with their friend, enjoying the work, and making money?

In living the dream of fame, you wonder what kind of legacy you will leave behind. One of the best compliments I could have received was from a *Family Feud* survey in the '80s. The question was something to the effect of "Name a popular professional wrestler." Hulk Hogan was first and I was second in front of Gorgeous George.

All in all, I was one damn lucky man.

CHAPTER 3

Living in Reality

I was managing in the Memphis territories during the '60s. At the time, I was the manager for the Masked Assassins, which, if you think about it, were two guys with white hoods. And we were in Arkansas. You don't think I was in trouble? I was a white guy who had a plastic rose in the lapel of his rented tux with white sunglasses. You don't think I was white meat and the fans didn't want to get at me?

When I got home, I got a check for $40. I told the promoter I couldn't go back because, as bizarre as it sounds, I couldn't afford it. He told me that I was suspended from the south. I wasn't too upset about it. The "Deliverance" fans would sit outside the building and drink whiskey in one hand and hold their shotguns with the other. When they got in the building, they would shoot the lights out over my head and would throw the bottles against the wall. And I'm in the ring with the hometown hero making 40 bucks before expenses.

That's the first time I thought, "Wow, this isn't what it's cracked up to be."

The first year I was in the business, Guy Mitchell—one of the Assassins that I managed—told me, "Kid, one day you're going to feel that this is the most rewarding thing you've ever done. You'll think that you're going to get a hundred bucks and you get 150," he said. "Then one day, kid, you're going to think, 'Why did I ever get into this?' because you're going to think you're going to get a hundred and you get 25."

"They say money can't buy happiness. Give me 50 bucks and watch me smile."

I didn't get it then because I was so caught up in the dream, but that was so true. You can't assume or expect anything in professional wrestling or life in general. Reality will wake you from that dream. While I was happy to get into wrestling back in the '60s, there were so many things that disappointed me about it.

Everybody is your friend when you first break into wrestling. I liked everyone and idolized everyone at first. But once you see them walking around the locker room naked, scratching their ass against the wall, that kind of takes the edge off. Then, you find out one guy doesn't like the other guy and then you discover that no one really likes anyone. They all laugh and act like they like each other, but they don't.

I am at least secure in knowing that I have a lot of good friends in this industry. There are so many of them.

I continued to work with the Assassins throughout the south, wrestling and doing television in Huntsville, Nashville, and Memphis. In Jonesboro, they would set the ring up and the police surrounding it would have blackjacks. Finally, it seemed like we'd have some kind of security and control. But they weren't even cops; they were 70-year-old members of the American Legion Police with the Boy Scout hats and uniforms that had about 1,700 badges attached. At the very least, they had more badges than teeth.

But it wasn't just the atmosphere of the south that shattered my dreams. The north wasn't much better. The first couple of years I worked in Chicago, I never made more than 50 bucks a shot. The Crusher stuck up for me once and told the promoter, "How can you pay the kid that?" The promoter would always say, "Well, he would make nothing if he wasn't working."

That was tough to deal with, but that was the mentality. Realizing that promoters never really cared about us shattered my dreams. I consider myself lucky that I've never been in the ring with a guy who deliberately wanted to hurt me. I was in the ring with guys who were clumsy enough, though, and they often did hurt me. But the fact of the matter was that the promoters—guys who, for the most part, never did what I did—never respected a manager in the business. They respected a wrestler.

The wrestlers respected me, but it was qualified. They would ask me, "Are you working tonight or managing?" which to them means that I was just sitting in the corner. I would simply respond, "I'm working," whether I was wrestling, managing, or both. The way I felt at the end of a match with all the aches, pains, and injuries, I was working. I would take more bumps than a lot of my men took during their match and they made $500 in the main event and I made $200. "You managed. He wrestled. He took the bumps," is what I would be told. What they did-n't realize was that "my wrestler" was out there and he took four bumps all night. I was out there for two minutes and took eight.

I tried to show them how hard I was busting my ass. I never sat on a chair when I managed at ringside. I wanted to be mobile. Plus, it's harder to hit a moving target as fans were throwing things at me, if I was up and moving around. I would tell my guys to lay the opponent's head over the bottom rope. I would take one step toward him. The fans would react. I would reach into my pocket. They'd scream at the referee that I had a foreign object. I'd take another step and pull my hand out. The ref-eree would ask me what I was doing. I'd show him my empty hand and say, "I'm not doing anything." He'd turn his back and walk away.

I'd walk by the wrestler lying on the bottom rope and slap him, which is a bigger insult than hitting someone. I would always have to ask in advance if I could slap him. A lot of guys don't like that, just like they don't like being kicked or patted on the ass. The referee would turn around and ask me what I was doing. Little things like that to show any-one who cared that I earned every dollar the promoters paid me.

But that's the way all promoters handled things. They thought a manager did less work than the wrestler. Respect is hard to come by, and you have to remember that even if you earn it by working hard, there will always be some who don't respect you because of what they think you do, not what you actually do.

I was discouraged for a long time and must admit that I'm still a lit-tle discouraged about it. I really wish I would have stuck up for myself more than I did. I know what my Wrestlemania 3 payoff was, and I know what Andre's payoff was. He made a lot more than me. In fact, he made right at or a little more than $1 million. There were three of us in the main event, including Hulk Hogan, and every man worked just as hard as the other.

If a promoter tells you that you're going to get so much and you don't, that again is "First Count" in action. The WWF claimed to have 93,000 people at the Pontiac Silverdome for Wrestlemania 3 in 1987. We don't know if there were 93,000 people. There could have been more, but I'm pretty sure there were no less. That's not how a promoter works. I worked for a promoter in Indianapolis that would tell us that the house was $10,000 to make us feel good. It was really $8,000, but he'd pay you based on $6,000. And there was probably a section of vet-erans who got in for free.

I always wondered that if I wasn't worth anything or even as much as a wrestler, why would they have me out there? All those years I put in and I always got less than the guys that I managed. That's why I managed differently—like a wrestler—so I could work the main events and make good money. Maybe in the end it made me a better manager, but that was my motivation, not theirs. I never knew what the guy I wrestled made, and I did not want to find out. If I was able to confirm that he got more than me, I'd be mad. On the other hand, if the wrestler I managed found out we made the same, he would bitch about it and go into his job all pissed off. And that's no way to go about doing your job, no matter if you're a professional wrestler or a dentist. Okay, especially if you're a dentist. There was no justice, and I began to realize that what I understood about the wrestling business was nothing. That was a big disappointment when I found out what people thought of me and managers overall.

No one ever understood I was never really a manager. I never "managed" anybody. And nobody ever "wrestled" anybody. You want to see wrestling, go to Iowa State. If you want to see professional wrestling, turn the television on or go to your local arena or Armory. We're all actors. I was just playing a role as a "manager." I portrayed a "wrestler" too. No one understood that, especially promoters. They were content to stay ignorant, just so they didn't have to pay you.

Promoters never appreciated anyone who went above and beyond the call of duty. They would just exploit it. It's about money to them, and a performer has to adopt that attitude too. It becomes less about love and passion and more about getting the payoff. I would wear a diamond tiara and a miniskirt to the ring if they paid me to. It was a job. I was an actor, plain and simple. If wrestling was real, I'd be selling shoes in a mall, looking up women's dresses.

The promoters never understood that I was often the cause of all the heat in the arena, even causing fans to riot. Dick the Bruiser used to tell me, "If anything ever goes wrong during a match, get in the ring and stay by me." His thought was to try to protect me if a fan ran into the ring. I was about two years in the business when he was wrestling Harley Race, who I was managing, in Milwaukee. Back then, it was a pretty wild town. The fans loved two things: drinking their beer and fighting the heels. Okay, three things if you count cheese. During the match, Bruiser was supposed to be knocked out cold and lay in the middle of the ring, getting heat on Harley. Well, the heat was on, and I was fanning the flames. Just doing my job. Fans started jumping up on the apron—in those days you didn't have security railings around the ring. Harley would try to keep them away by running over to the closest fan and, one by one, knock each one out cold as they jumped up to the ring.

Meanwhile, Bruiser was selling the knockout and still laying down. Some moron in the back who was in charge of the lighting decided it would be a good idea to turn off every light in the building. I was sitting at ringside, watching the fans coming, until the moron shut off the lights. All I could think of was Bruiser telling me, "If anything ever goes wrong, kid, get in the ring and stay by me."

When the lights came back up, there I was, laying next to Bruiser on the mat with his arm draped over me. And if I had a blanky, I would have probably been holding onto it while sucking my thumb.

As I gained more experience in the business and pissed off the fans even more, I stopped taking that crap from them. You think the fans would be there to enjoy the show because they enjoyed what we did. Maybe they enjoyed it too much or took it too seriously. When you think of being famous, you think of adoring fans who want autographs and pictures, not the fans I had back then. Now, they weren't all bad, but I realized early in my career that I would do anything to just get them back a little bit if they took a swing at me or spit on me.

I was working a wrestling show one night in Denver, which was a real wild town with energetic fans who would always sell the buildings out. After the match, I had to make the extremely long walk back to the dressing room with people spitting on me and throwing beers at me. I had a routine when I would walk back into the dressing room, I would shake every cop's hand and thank them. Whether people like police or not, you don't call your brother-in-law when there is trouble, you call the cops. Someone does something to your kid, you don't call the milkman, you call the cops. But when you get pulled over for doing 60 in a 50 mile-per-hour zone, you get mad at them and wonder what the hell they're doing there. Remember, it's your job to obey the law or try to out-smart them. It's their job to catch you.

One night, after I greeted all the Denver cops, I saw this kid in the dressing room in handcuffs. Apparently, he was the one spitting on me and some other guys. That wasn't enough for handcuffs, but then he hit a cop. The cop next to him said, "Sit there on that bench and don't move," and he handcuffed him. As the cop was leaving, I decided to have a little fun. I told the cop, "Officer, that kid just gave you the finger." The cop went back and beat him unmercifully while he was still hand-cuffed. How could he give a cop the finger? Well, he spit on me and I got back at him. I don't think the kid will ever do that again.

In Omaha, Nebraska, they were throwing all kinds of crap in the ring. The cops found a guy who was doing it and brought him back to the dressing room. Nick Bockwinkel and I took matters into our own hands and brought the guy into the dressing room. Nick walked into the shower and turned it on while still wearing his trunks and boots. He grabbed the guy by the tie and pulled him in there with him. Nick yelled at the guy and asked him who he thought he was, spitting and throwing punches at us. The guy stood there with all this water pouring on him in his street clothes. I hope he learned his lesson better than he could keep himself dry. The only thing he could do is put his right hand over his left pocket to keep his cigarettes dry.

Just like any job that anyone would hold, there would sometimes be a change of employers. For me, a major change came when I was working for the NWA down in Georgia. I started in February of 1979, managing Blackjack Lanza. When Jack left the promotion for Minneapolis in May, I felt like I was stuck in Georgia and didn't know what to do. My mother had died in April and my wife and daughter—who wasn't even a year old—were back in Indianapolis. I went to the booker—the guy in charge of everything—and said, "Well, Jack's gone now. Do you want me to manage another guy or leave?"

"No," he said. "I'll put you with the Masked Superstar and 'Killer' Karl Kox."

I asked him, "How long do I have here?"

He said, "You're here however long you want to be here."

I felt secure as anyone would in that situation. When your employer tells you that you have long-term employment you believe them. But things change. Nowadays, people are laid off without warning because a company is losing money or they may want to increase their cash flow. The quickest way is to cut employees. For me, it was just a promoter's whim when in October of that same year, he gave me my notice to finish up.

The sad thing is that I had bought a house in June.

He told me I was making too much money. I was making between $900 and $1,200 a week, and the promoter didn't want to pay that any more for "just" a manager.

Wrestling can be just like any other profession. We all can relate to the employer telling us we're out of line with their budget and making more than we should be making.

The night before the big Thanksgiving show, the booker sent me to wrestle Tommy Rich in Valdosta, Georgia. It was 500 miles round trip and I made 50 bucks for the spot show. I was finishing up anyway and never missed a shot the entire time I was in the NWA. I worked hard there. Why didn't they just give me the night off? My whole time there, I had two nights off in a year.

I finished up on Thanksgiving night in 1979 wrestling Tommy Rich in a cage match at the Omni. The place was sold out, probably close to 20,000 people. What did I make for that night? Fifteen hundred bucks.

That may not sound bad, until you realize that Tommy Rich probably got $3,000 for the same match and the same amount of time.

You know why my soon-to-be former boss gave me that? Because I was leaving. On top of that, I was wrestling and not "just managing." What could I bitch about? Am I not going to show up the next night? They had me by the you-know-what. I couldn't bitch, go into business for myself, or refuse to ever work for them, because I was on my way out the door. The employer controlled everything. It was a reality I had to face, and my suggestion is for everyone to face that reality, too. It's a balance between pride and reputation. Plus, I had to make a living in the future to support my family. I really didn't have a choice.

Those experiences truly burst my bubble. They lied to me about having a job as long as I wanted, and I couldn't do anything about it. They made me travel hundreds of miles for low pay because they knew they could. Now I don't mind if somebody punches me if I can get a shot at them. But I don't want to be "snipered"—somebody hitting me and I can't get to them. And that's what happened to me.

Maybe I should have complained, but my problem was that I acted like a professional and they took advantage of that. My eyes were opened.

Wrestlers weren't respected or treated fairly, and there was no consistency in payment. You'd get minimum pay to start, and it would get better as you got more experience and moved up the card. But the promoter would never tell you what you would eventually get paid. There was no chart, manual, or book. There was no union, and I didn't have an agent. They kept everyone broke and that took away the incentive to move from promotion to promotion. You'd make the same from one end of the country to another. Now if they gave you a grand a week, you could afford to pick up and move. But that didn't happen back then.

The difference between a main-event guy and a lower-level guy was significant. In St. Paul or Chicago, guys in the main event made $1,000. First match guys would make $75 to $100.

I was fortunate in that the pay scale allowed me to not have to work every day. Not bad for someone who was not educated beyond the eighth grade. I essentially worked nights. If I was working in a regular territory, I wouldn't have to get up until 5:00 in the afternoon. Some guys never bothered to go to bed. I remember Ray Stevens telling me in 1978 that he hadn't been to bed since 1952. And I believed him. Then again, he was the kind of guy who would go out for a loaf of bread for his wife and be gone for two weeks. When he would come back, all his wife would say was, "Where's the bread?"

If you're not enjoying your job and you're getting paid well, you've got to weigh certain things. Do you want happiness or money and benefits for your family? In the end, if you don't like your job, look for something else. If you can't because you have nine kids, to be honest, you should have bought nine condoms. You have to be careful and not get yourself in those situations. Think ahead of how family affects your work and vice versa. And if you didn't, then it is your obligation to do what you have to do to support your family. I'm not knocking anyone who has kids accidentally, because it happens to a lot of people, both good and bad. But some people just get themselves stuck.

In many ways, I felt stuck toward the end of my time in the AWA. I saw people like Hulk Hogan and Gene Okerlund going to the WWF, making money, and being part of something special. Signing with the WWF and living that life was great, but the travel was an eye-opening, bubble-bursting pain in the ass and reality check. They would fly me to England for a pay-per-view. But I wouldn't fly directly there. I would fly to Manchester and have drive to Sheffield—on the wrong side of the road, mind you—so Monsoon and I could do announcing for the show.

Leading up to that and within a time span of six days, I flew from Tampa to New York so Curt Hennig, "Hacksaw" Jim Duggan, and I could fly on the Concord to England for some interviews and a press conference. The next day, we flew to Munich, Germany, for another set of interviews and a press conference. Then we flew to Rotterdam, Holland, and took a car to Amsterdam for another press conference. The next day, we were in Milan, Italy for another press conference. We flew out from there the next morning to Bermuda. From there we flew to Atlanta and eventually ended up in Mobile, Alabama for a show that night. Yes, I got to travel the world, but I hardly saw any of those countries outside of their airports.

Your job may be a dream, but in the end, it is also your job. The good, the bad, and the ugly. For me, the ugly was traveling, and traveling overseas was as ugly and challenging as anything I've ever experienced.

The best advice I can give to anyone traveling is four simple words: peanut butter and jelly. You can get to any country and always find bread and crackers, but you can't always find meat, fish, or anything to eat for that matter. Sometimes you don't even know what you're getting and the lunchmeat looks like the north end of a southbound dachshund. But I do recommend the Wendy's in Milan that serves wine with your Biggie Fries.

In all honestly, I loved Italy, so it wasn't all ugly. People were very polite there. My wife and I went to Harrah's department store. This woman got to the door a few seconds before we did and opened it for us. I thanked her and turned to my wife.

"Isn't that nice? They do the same thing in New York, you know. I saw a woman open a door for another woman, but two of her kids went through her purse while the other woman was holding it."

For all the good, there was disappointment everywhere. In broadcasting, I loved working with people like Gorilla Monsoon, Vince McMahon, and Jim Ross in the WWF. But then there were people at WCW who just made going to work intolerable. It wasn't fun anymore. I don't like doing anything unless its fun. I really don't. Some people work 12 to 14 hours a day as bricklayers. I saw movers move me I don't know how many times around the country. Those guys are extremely strong and never stop working. And they very well could be having fun. God knows I made my own fun, no matter what the situation or setting. But I could never do what those guys do for a living. Remember the laziness. There are people who work hard for less money than I ever made.

Some people live in Minnesota and other cold and snowy states and make money. My advice to them is that they can live in the warm weather and make money and not have to shovel snow and be indoors half the year. Don't get me wrong. It's a beautiful state. People respect their properties and there is a lot of culture, but it's damn cold.

I was staying at a Holiday Inn in Des Moines, Iowa. It was 35 below. I walked in and asked the woman at the desk, "Are there any Holiday Inns in San Diego?"

She said, "Yes."

I shot back, "Why aren't you there? Why are you here? Its 11 at night, ma'am and you're 70 years old. It's 35 below!"

"We have full-service gas stations."

"Jesus Christ," I said. "I'm moving here."

Full-service gas stations. Now that's reality.

CHAPTER 4

Knowing Yourself

One night during the time I was working in Atlanta in 1979, I was staring at my wrestling jacket that had "California" written on the back of it. It got me to thinking.

Ole Anderson was standing close by. I walked up to him, pointed at my jacket and said, "Look at that. Do you realize what I do? If I had to go to a psychiatrist and he asked me what I did for a living, I'd say I manage a man who I don't really manage and he claims that he's a wrestler, but he's not really a wrestler. He claims he's from Albuquerque, New Mexico, but he's really from Minneapolis, Minnesota.

"My name is Ray Heenan, but I was named 'Bobby' by Dick the Bruiser. To this day, I'm not 100 percent sure why. I have 'California' written across my back. Never been there. I bleached my hair and changed my name to 'Pretty Boy.' I have no idea why. I know I'm straight.

"If you ask me how much I make a night, I'd say, 'I have no idea yet. I know what I made last week and I think I got it, but I don't know what I'll make this week yet.' In my pocket, I have a half a piece of soap with tape around it, pretending I'm carrying a weapon. The soap and tape are made in America, but it still makes a 'foreign object.' In the other pocket, I'm carrying a Gillette blade, broke in half with taped wrapped around it too, in case I want to cut my head.

"The psychiatrist would put me in one of those jackets with the sleeves in the back and lock me up.

"But that's what I do for a living."

"Some people are at a disadvantage when they wake up."

One of my philosophies in life is that you know yourself. My suggestion to everyone is to videotape yourself. For example, when you play golf, you don't know how your swing is unless you get a chance to see it. You don't know how you are in life unless you have the chance to watch yourself and see what you do. My mother never knew how silly and funny she was. I wish she had seen what I saw. I probably don't really know how I am either, even though my character was often on television. But that was my character. On the other hand, some people don't know how mean they are, how bad they are, how cheap they are, or how rude they are, unless they see themselves.

Seeing what you do can change you, but unless you have an open mind, you can't correct. A lot of people make excuses for what they do. They blame someone else, never themselves. I don't buy that. You do what you want to do because you do it. If I reacted violently toward my wife every time she upset me, me and OJ would have shared a cell.

A lot of people will tell you to know yourself, but that's a hard thing to do. You're not objective when you try to see who you are. Others can give you their opinions, but if you don't like what they say, you shut down and don't listen to them. That's why videotape can be objective. Videotape yourself at home. Videotape yourself at work. That's a great way just to get to know yourself, the person you spend the most time with.

Thinking about my job, I never really knew what my job description was, if I had one in the first place. At least a clown can say, "I'm Flippo the Flying Clown. That's what he is. He wears face paint and makes kids laugh, kind of like the Ultimate Warrior. I'm a manager. Of who? No one. And who was I really and what did I do? That depended on who you asked.

In the early '90s, I had to testify before the grand jury when Vince McMahon was under investigation for steroid distribution. I brought my attorney, Michael Labram, with me who also has a talk show for WABC radio in New York under the name "Lionel."

I went to Brooklyn to give a deposition at the District Attorney's office. I simply told them the truth in that I knew nothing about steroid use. There were people who looked like they might have taken them, but I never saw anyone inject themselves or swallow anything. I've never heard or seen Vince sell them to anyone. I wasn't about muscles and steroids. I was about laughing, entertainment, and laziness. I didn't like to work out. For those who went to the gym and took steroids, that was their business, not mine. They're grown men, just maybe a little too "grown."

I walked into the grand jury room. There were 12 jurors and three judges sitting there. I walked up to the stand, was sworn in, and sat down. The rule was that if the attorneys and judges wanted to ask each other something, I would have to leave the room. And if I wanted to talk to my attorney, I could leave the room, because he couldn't be in there with me.

As I sat on the witness stand, the District Attorney asked me a bunch of questions for the deposition.

"Who did you manage?" he asked.

"Well, I didn't really manage."

"What did you do then, Mr. Heenan?"

"I pretended I managed," I told him honestly.

"Who handles their money?"

"McMahon."

"Don't you handle their money?"

"No," I said.

"Who handles their booking?"

"McMahon."

"But you're their manager?"

"Yes."

The attorney paused.

"Mr. Heenan. Could you please leave the room?"

I got up and walked out of the room. After a little while, they had me come back and take the stand again.

The district attorney said, "Let me get this right. Who handles all the wrestlers' airplane reservations?"

"Titan Sports," I said.

"Who handles their room reservations?"

"Titan Sports."

"What did you do?"

"I was the manager."

"Do you do anything for the wrestlers?"

"Not a damn thing."

He asked me to leave the room again. I went back into the room after a while and noticed that the jury was now laughing. I sat back down on the stand.

"How long have you been doing this?" the attorney asked me.

"Practically all my life and I've never been really sure what I do. I'm not sure if I manage. You know something? I don't really wrestle. I prefer managing, because I get to wear clothes."

"You don't wear clothes when you wrestle?" he asked.

"I wear wrestling clothes."

"Then, you wrestle?"

"No. Not at all."

"Because you're a manager?"

"I'm not really a manager."

"Well, what's your job title then?"

"I'm a manager."

"Are you a broadcaster too?"

"Yes."

"What do you broadcast?"

"Wrestling."

"Would you please leave the room again?" he asked me.

"Could this be the last time?" I asked back. "My knees are killing me."

I went out again and then came back. My attorney came back in with me and said to the judges, "Am I right? I told you he knows nothing."

They let me go. I shook the DA's hand. "Thank you, Perry Mason," I said as I left.

Manager or no manager, sometimes I literally didn't even know my own name.

When I first worked for the AWA in Minneapolis, I was managing—well, you know what I mean—Harley Race in Indiana. He tagged with Larry Hennig, but Hennig tore his knee and they were going to use Harley as a singles wrestler. I knew Wally Karbo and Verne Gagne, who ran the AWA, from working with them in Chicago, and they had an idea to bring me in to manage Harley for a month. It was a great break for me. I was 23 years old, and it was my first big trip away from home on an airplane. I was in a different territory, but I was comfortable in that I already knew a lot of the guys from working in Chicago. But the bottom line was I was going to manage Harley Race and make some money.

I took a cab to the Dikeman Hotel where the AWA offices were located. I got up to the promoter's office on the sixth floor. In that office, there were pictures of all these wrestlers on the wall. There were glass windows and a secretary right in front. It was an impressive sight. I saw Wally Karbo's and Verne Gagne's offices and their desks. I saw another room with television tapes and magazines. It looked like a stereotypical promoter's office. Just what I imagined it would be.

I greeted Wally when he came out into the lobby. "Oh, hi Bobby," he said. "Verne and I are in the office having a meeting. We'll be right with you."

He started to leave, but then turned around and told me, "But, for the time being, don't tell anybody who you are. I don't know if we're going to call you Bobby Heenan, Ray Heenan, Bobby Race, or Ray Race."

Now from time to time, a wrestling fan would come up to see if the wrestlers were in the office or to buy pictures. This kid comes in while I'm sitting there and recognizes me. He asks, "Can I have your autograph?"

I said, "As soon as I know who I am."

CHAPTER 5

Knowing Your Limitations, When to Shut Up, and When to Walk Away

I don't have anything motorized except my car. I don't own a motorcycle or anything like that. Too many things can go wrong and I'd have to call someone to fix it. I can't fix anything. I told my wife once that I can fix anything by just calling someone in the Yellow Pages.

Vince McMahon used to say, "Every match you have is closer to your last."

He's right. A lot of guys think that their wrestling career will never end. But when it is over and they may not have saved a whole lot of money, they have to work for a living doing another job. Now they'll claim that in professional wrestling, they've worked for a living all their life, working hard in that ring and traveling around the world. But after that, they have to work for a living at Sears and lift refrigerators. They have to go and take out sewage. They have to clean urinals.

These guys enjoyed being in the dressing rooms and bars and hanging around with the boys. I think we spent more time in the locker room and the bar than we did in front of the audience. It's camaraderie whether you like the guys or not.

"The two things that scare me most about wrestling fans is that they're allowed to vote and allowed to reproduce."

I think the reason a lot of the guys hang on in this business is because it's all they've ever done and it's all they can do. Plus, its quick money. They don't have to work a week to make a hundred bucks. They can make $50 to $100 in just one night. And it still gets them a little recognition and pride.

I figure a lot of guys continue to wrestle well past their prime because they need the money, and their second and third wives have the money they made before. That's why some guys are still wrestling. It's all they can do. You're not going to see most wrestlers working at Radio Shack, Pizza Hut, or even Dunn and Bradstreet. Chances are they're not going to be a doctors, lawyers, accountants, or pizza delivery guys. What can they do? Wrestle and entertain.

It's what they do best. Men up there in age with limited education don't have a lot of job options out there. Even if they do, they could also have a love and dedication for this business that simply won't die.

But sometimes you have to let it die. You have to let it go. They say that quitters never win and winners never quit. That's not quite accurate. There are situations where you have to know when to say goodbye to something. You've maybe worn out your welcome or you just can't do it as well as you once could. Age sneaks up on you. Your skills deteriorate. You're limited, and you have to recognize those limitations.

When the WWF was really going big time in the '80s, they made the decision for a lot of the guys who were maybe past their prime. They just stopped using guys who usually wrestled on the big shows and made them jobbers or preliminary guys on television. The older guys made way for the new generation of *Rock and Wrestling*. But it was funny. They didn't care. They were just looking to stay on and hold on to that brass ring as long as they could. The business just passed them by, but they were wrestlers through and through.

"Spaceman" Frank Hickey was this wrestler who wore a big cape and leather helmet and it made him look like a spaceman that you'd see in an old movie. While he loved wrestling, his dream was always to be in the circus. When someone would backdrop him during a match, he would say, "shot out of the cannon" to no one but himself. He loved the circus. He would go there every chance he could—sometimes every day—before the circus would open to watch the guys set up. He never was married. And I don't think he made a whole lot of money.

Frank was a strange man. He would put newspapers on the dressing room floor and spray the entire room with Lysol. If he had to wrestle under a mask, he would drive twenty miles out of town and into a forest before he took his mask off as if the fans were following him. No one cared, but we didn't tell Frank that.

He was so unusual and so funny. He would just say funny things like "Furnam and Durnam" for absolutely no reason and "Pepper Tree," because this promoter would have a pepper tree outside of his office where the boys would gather around and gossip. Frank would say that to let them know he saw them gossiping. He'd talk about his conversations with the bunnies and the rabbits. He would call everyone "goof." "Hello, goof," he would say in a funny little voice.

He even had little sayings. When someone real successful in the business and maybe didn't do enough to deserve it—like Dick the Bruiser—would walk past him, he would say, "Dick the Bruiser: Too much, too soon. Frank Hickey: Too long, not enough."

He would tease me and say, "I know what you want. You don't want to go to school and get an education. No! You don't want to get a good job. No! You want to bleach your hair and get a Cadillac, a six pack, and an arena rat."

He invited me to the hotel one day because he desperately wanted to show me something. I got there, and there was Frank, sitting by his 1955 Cadillac with solid steel floorboards. He was reading a book with the trunk open and all his helmets and capes on displays. He just wanted to show me that.

A day with Frank was interesting to say the least. We were flying to Winnipeg one day in 1969. Frank was wearing a suit that looked like it belonged to Al Capone, and it smelled like mothballs. My grandfather had to have made it. He brought this trunk onto the plane with a belt tied around it to keep it shut. He tried to shove it into the overhead, but the stewardess stopped him and said, "You can't put that up there."

Frank said, "They let me put that on the 'Hound'."

Then, Larry Hennig walked up to Frank and asked him, "Frank, where did you get the suit made?"

"In Japan," he said.

"When the hell were you in Japan?" Larry asked.

"1921."

I got off the plane and Frank pulled me aside. "Mr. Heenan? Mr. Hickey, FBI."

He grabbed my arm and walked with me.

"What does FBI mean?" I asked.

"Fucking big idiot."

He showed me a letter from his girlfriend. It would say, "I hate you. I can't stand the sight of you. You're a big fat pig. Don't ever call me when you come to town again."

He would hand me the letter and whine, "What does this mean?"

I would say, "Frank, she is playing hard to get."

"Do you think she wants me to get her flowers?"

When I started in the '60s, I swear Frank had to be 60. Promoters used him on television as a favor to him. But he was getting heavy—probably about 300 pounds—and his knees were shot. He had the opportunity to wrestle Verne Gagne once. Verne put him in the sleeper hold and "put him to sleep."

With the match over, Verne jumped out the ring to do an interview. As he talked, Frank started snoring loudly in the ring. Verne said to Wally, "What the hell is going on here. Get him out of the ring."

Verne asked Frank later, "What the hell were you doing?"

Frank looked him in the eye and said, "When you sleep, you snore."

If a guy would land on him too hard, he would say, "Time for school." He'd show you how to do it without hurting you. But in the end, he stayed on too long in his career. I was concerned for his health because of his weight and because he was an older man. Frank would always ask me, "Could you get me booked any place, Bobby?"

Later on, he informed me that Vince McMahon Sr. offered him a job in the New York office. All he had to do was come in and handle the mail and answer phones. They would give him so much money a week and put him up in an apartment in Washington, D.C.

I was so happy for him. Here was his chance to stay in the business. I told him, "Frank, that is wonderful. I hope that when it's my time to end my career, someone thinks enough of me and offers me a lifetime job. I think you should do it."

He said, "I'm going to call Bruno Sammartino and work in Pittsburgh."

He meant to wrestle. At that point, I had to be honest. "Frank, it's over. You're not going to make any money anymore. You're going to get hurt. The promoters are like pimps, and we're like whores. When Shirley breaks her ankle and can't walk that street, she's on the shelf, just like us. They'll find someone new with a bubble ass and a short dress. Frank, you'll break your ankle and you don't have a bubble ass."

More than anything, I wanted to convince Frank to stop wrestling. "Frank, take the offer that Vince Sr. gave you. It's an offer out of compassion and care."

He paused and thought about it. "But I'm a wrestler," he said.

He wouldn't listen. I heard that eventually Frank moved to Tennessee and wound up working for a wrestler named Herb Larson in a hotel. He was a janitor.

That was his life. Wrestling and the circus. He loved them both so much.

Frank Hickey died on December 8, 1995. The Jarretts used him a few years before that. He jumped at the opportunity. They arranged a place to meet Frank to pick him up. When they got there, Frank was waiting in his wheelchair, holding onto his bag and wearing his helmet and cape.

The storyline was that a wrestler needed a partner and told the crowd, "I'll get 'Spaceman' Frank Hickey." He walked backstage and brought Frank out in a wheelchair. Frank was able to get up long enough to stand on the apron. He was crippled and old, but he loved being in front of the crowd. And they loved him.

I loved him, too. He was great. If I had a territory and Frank was still alive, I'd use him in some capacity. Just to keep the boys loose.

There were a lot of good guys in the territories who would make you laugh. You don't want to be around a bunch of Ultimate Warriors. You want to be around a bunch of Bobby Heenans, Curt Hennigs, Ray Stevens, and, yes, Frank Hickeys.

There was no shame in Frank walking away. He would have won by quitting. It's a lesson for all of us. I know that I can't do what I did when I was younger. I can't and don't want to wrestle or manage anymore. And, in spite of shattered dreams and advising people reading this book to stay away from professional wrestling, I still love this business as much as I did as a child. I'm just more realistic. But I still want to contribute and see the fans.

After I left WCW and was diagnosed with cancer, many independent wrestling promotions asked me to come work for them. At first, I thought it seemed like I was going from the Academy Awards to the state fair and it would be a step down. Mainly, I was also worried about staying on past my prime as I had watched so many do. But after doing it, I realized that it was fun. Who else can say that they've done everything in their professional life? I would love to continue doing it. After all, I've already worked in barns, tents, carnivals, and fairs. I also worked in Madison Square Garden and the Pontiac Silverdome. I don't care about the wrestling end of it so much or even the quality. I like to see young wrestlers go out to that ring and give it a try. It's just fun to be there and get out of the house.

Don't get me wrong. I don't want to wrestle in the ring or manage anymore. I have no desire to be in the ring and get bounced around. I enjoy going to the independent shows, signing a few autographs, and talking to the fans.

It reminds me a bit of the old days, more so than the so-called "big shows" I was a part of throughout my career. The guys out there are really trying, and the fans seem to really enjoy it. It's the kind of night where you can go out and not have to mortgage your house to pay for the tickets.

I learned that there is a difference in overstaying your welcome and just enjoying your visit. I don't want to steal the spotlight from anyone or have a local guy put me over in a match just because I'm Bobby Heenan. I want to help out where I can and draw some money for these guys. Hopefully, "First Count" doesn't exist anymore.

But I doubt it.

In many ways, playing more of a supporting role at the independent shows and helping the guys out has helped me to realize that I have limitations in the business. I can't bump and I don't want to. Actually, I've had limitations throughout my entire career. We all do, no matter what stage we are in of our career or what type of position we're holding. Challenges are fine, but we should also know when a challenge is becoming too challenging. Winners never quit? Well, judge for yourself.

Many fans don't know this, but I held a position of power once in what was then known as the WWF around 1985. I was the assistant booker with George Scott, who was the head booker. Yes, "The Brain" was third in command for the largest wrestling organization in the world, if you think about it. The wrestlers were finally sucking up to me because of the title and the perceived power. But what they didn't know was that I had nothing to do. I didn't last long in that job. Mainly because George thought I didn't know what to do. He was right. The fact was that I didn't know what to do because he never told me what to do. My main job was reading fan mail all day.

I got the job after I approached Vince McMahon about an idea for the Missing Link, a guy I was managing. He had a caveman gimmick and never talked. He had a hell of a body with a painted green face. I said, "Vince, he doesn't go into the ring in the right way." My problem with him was that he was always trying to run his own head in the post, going nuts, and screaming his head off.

I told Vince that we should put emphasis on this guy, or he would look like just another guy who works at a hot dog stand in New York, painted face or not. I suggested something different for him.

My idea was to come to the ring with the Link, but there would be no Link with me. I would walk back to the dressing room, stay back there for a minute, and then come back out. Still, no Link. I would get on the microphone, "Will someone in the back send the Link out if you can find him?"

I would go to the back and "look for the Link" again. Everyone in the building was standing and looking in the entryway for him, drawing more attention to his character. I would again come back, but this time he was with me. I'd yell "Come on, come on." He eventually got in the ring and wrestled. The delay was effective, because you don't want the Link to go more than 10 minutes anyway in an actual match, because all he did was fly around the ring like a maniac. It got old after awhile. I think we realized his limitations and played to his strengths.

Vince liked the idea, and we incorporated it into the Link's entrance. I guess he liked it so much, and it worked so well that he approached me to be the assistant booker under George.

All I wanted to do was help out. I didn't want George's job, but maybe he thought I did. Again, he wasn't giving me much to do, because he didn't think I could do anything. But I couldn't do anything, because I wasn't sure what to do. That was a tremendous limitation. I guess other employers will do that to you as well. They'll feel threatened for whatever reason and do what they can to hold their employees back. The simple advice is to say, "Don't let them." But I handled the situation a bit differently and knew when I had enough.

I was in the office a couple of days a week when I wasn't on the road. In my desk, I had a scissors and a thumbtack. That was it. They would pay me the same as they would have on the road. So, instead of traveling, paying for my room and rental car, the office paid for my hotel and transportation and gave me the money I would have made if I had been traveling.

Vince even lent me his Lincoln to drive around town. He invited me to stay at his home, but I decided a hotel would be better. Now I didn't mind being in the office two to three days a week to help out, but I wasn't helping anyone. I didn't like reading all that fan mail. Do you know how many letters in crayon a man can read from wrestling fans? Not many when they sound something like this:

Dear Mr. Bruno Sammartino:
I want you to kill King Kong Bundy.
Folded that up in a ball and threw it in a wastepaper can.

Hulk Hogan:
You are my favorite. I love you.
Signed,
Vince.

I even got my own letters. One girl from Fresno kept writing me, telling me about how much her eyebrow pencil and lipstick would cost her. She thanked me for being at her home the night before and asked me if I liked her negligee. She'd go on and on about how I parked my car in front of her house and the neighbors got mad about it. She would tell me she bought a new wig and new outfits. I never met this woman in my whole life.

Then, she sent me a picture of her. I swear she looked like a fat Dusty Rhodes. And Dusty Rhodes weighs 350 pounds. She was blonde, around 50, and had to be at least 400 pounds. She had these huge funbags that if you lifted them up, you could see the word Everlast.

Those were the types of fans I drew. That's the kind of fan mail I got. Others had gorgeous women stalking them, following them to their hotel rooms, and generally had them falling at their feet. Me? I got the female "American Dream."

That's not as bad as the fan who sent me a shoebox with a Kotex, a hot dog, and a jar of mayonnaise. The promoter looked at it and said, "I'm a little concerned with the clientele you're drawing."

I never discussed anything with George. No one would tell me anything that I needed to discuss, so I did very little. I'd show up to the office in a shirt and tie and read fan mail. I would go out to lunch with some people and then I would come back and read some more fan mail. To break things up a little, I would run an errand from time to time. Sometimes, I was asked to call one of the wrestlers to tell him he had to make a town because someone called in sick. My day ended at five and I would go back to my hotel room.

Just sitting there all day drove me nuts. There was absolutely nothing creative about being the assistant booker, which was supposed to be a creative position. I just went through boxes and boxes of fan mail. Keep in mind that the WWF was very popular in those days.

After two weeks—or maybe it was less, I'm still trying to block that whole experience from my mind—I just went back home to Florida. The job wasn't fun, and I was tired of reading letters. It all started when I showed some creativity, but ended when there was nothing that required creativity, except how to use a letter opener. If I continued in that job, I would have used it on myself.

To show how valuable my contribution was to them, it actually took a month for anyone to realize that I was gone. They never missed me at that office. Vince called me one day.

"Where are you?"

"I went home," I answered.

"Well, George said you didn't know what you were doing," Vince said.

"I didn't know what I was doing. That's why I went home."

We all need to know when it is a good time to stand up and a good time to just walk away. If someone promises you a certain kind of job and they don't deliver, call them on it. But if you feel you're hitting a brick wall, save your sanity. Take the letter opener away from your throat and just walk away. There's no shame in it. I wish others would have realized their limitations and just knew when enough was enough.

People can be in their prime and not recognize limitations and boundaries. That's important in professional wrestling. There are many unwritten rules and you have to learn respect. Timing is very important as well, not just in wrestling, but in life. When I started, most of the guys knew me because I set up the ring and carried jackets. I didn't have to gain acceptance. By the time I went to another territory, I was already in the business for a couple of years, so the guys there knew who I was. I never had the problem of being an unknown guy. My timing was usually right.

I've seen guys come into the dressing room and they don't learn when to keep their mouths shut. They'd talk to a veteran like they've been in the business for a long time or have known them all their life. Remember the old saying of familiarity breeding contempt? I sure learned the hard way.

There was a tag team called the Von Brauns. I was new in the business when I met them in a dressing room in Louisville, Kentucky. In professional wrestling, we would always call each other by our gimmicks, not our real names. That way, you never used someone's real name in public.

I found out after riding in the car to the show with Guy Mitchell, that one of the Von Brauns was actually a friend of his named Doug Donovan.

We were in the dressing room. Doug politely said hi to me and I said, "Hi Doug."

He immediately called me in the showers. "Don't call me by my first name again," he said sternly. "Call me by my gimmick." I never called anybody by their real name again. I was very careful of that. Only my closest friends will I call by their real names, but some guys in the business still don't like it, no matter what.

I could see the looks in some guys' eyes when some new guy talked big. I'll guarantee you that he was going to end up getting stuck with the hotel or bar bill, get coffee for everyone, or get a few potatoes in the ring, which means getting hit legitimately hard. Ever have someone throw a raw potato at you? It hurts. That's why they call it that. Or maybe, if a guy didn't respect those boundaries, he would be made out to look like a fool. When he came back from the ring, his ass would be cut out of his pants, a sock was missing, or one of his shoes was gone. Or maybe both were glued to the floor.

"Hey, you don't know me that well," is what they'll always say and if that's to put a guy in his place, that's fine.

We all need to be put in our place. That teaches us that we have boundaries and limitations, no matter how successful or comfortable we all are. No shame in walking away to save face, save embarrassment, or stop reading fan/love letters day in and day out.

I still wonder whatever happened to "Dusty."

CHAPTER 6

Chair Shots and Lies and Other Setbacks

I'*ve done a lot of radio and television interviews since the first book came out. I'd often get asked if I was ever hit over the head with a chair. I would tell them, "I've been hit so many times over the head with a chair, the top of my head smells like ass."*

When a chair connects with a wrestler's head or any other part of his or her body, that's a chair shot. For this book, think of a chair shot as a speed bump in life. We all get hit with chairs sometimes, figuratively speaking, outside of the wrestling ring. We all face speed bumps. For me, it happened with my cancer and it happened growing up. Nobody goes through life with everything being a "10." It's not going to rain today. The check will be in the mailbox. The boss will give me a raise. My wife loves me. The kids are getting all As.

Life just doesn't happen like that. There's a chair with your name waiting for you from time to time.

We're human. Actually, we're mammals. We're kind of like dogs that talk and stand on two feet. In fact, dogs may be smarter. Who is it that has to take them out for a walk and pick up their shit? They're leaving piles of chair shots.

"My advice is like Jell-O. There is always room for more."

We all have chair shots in life. You can't let it get to you, because as soon as you get over something, something else is going to happen. Multiple chair shots. That's just the way it is. If you worry about those chair shots you can't control, that will kill you. Worry about those chair shots that you can control and see coming. After all, how many things can you control in your life? Can you control your income? Yes, if you do a good job, but that may not matter. A new boss could come in and a new broom will sweep everything clean. You can save all your money and invest it well and the stock market crashes. That's another chair shot and you lose everything. You date this beautiful girl and you're having a great, romantic relationship. Then, she gets pregnant. That's more than a chair shot. That's a groin shot, pal. Then, you get over the shock and you want a boy, but it turns out to be a girl. Or you get used to the idea of having one baby and it turns out to be triplets.

Life is like that, but you have to condition yourself to be able to take those chair shots. If you can't and you're a defeatist, there's nothing left for you to gain. People will beat you with chairs constantly, so you have to tell yourself that you're better than that, self-esteem is important. You don't need a lot, just enough to get through life and not piss off the people who are holding those chairs.

But sometimes those chairs will connect, and the best thing you can do is never let someone who is trying to hurt you know that you're hurt. You're at your worst when you admit that you're wounded. You're going to get hurt a lot in this life by people you wouldn't suspect were capable of such things.

I never get mad and I never get even. Oh, I get hurt. When someone does something to me that isn't right, I'm hurt. People who I thought were friends of mine ended up just looking out for themselves. That hurts more than anything, including a chair shot.

I'd rather be hit over the head by a chair from an irate wrestling fan than take one in the gut from a friend of mine. The pain I feel from the fan hitting me will go away. But the memory of a friend hurting me or betraying me will always stay with me. I have strong ties to my friends, and friendship means a lot to me. I gained a reputation throughout my career for bleeding. That's where I bleed the most.

You can't let it bother you or consume you. Don't let anyone get the better of you just because they are willing to sink lower than you. Sometimes you have to write down on a piece of paper your assets and your liabilities. Assets being your friends, for example, and liabilities being those chair shots. When I met my wife, she wrote down all of her liabilities—every bill she owed on and anything else she could think of.

Then, she turned the paper over and put down her biggest asset. She wrote, "One big asshole." In case you haven't guessed, that's me.

For every good, there is bad and for every bad, there is good. Look at that garbage pile of life and pick out what you want. People eat out of dumpsters and in fancy restaurants. Some people drink champagne while others drink out of toilets. We're human. And it's what you make out of your life. If you think you're going to drink out of a toilet, you probably will. It's hard for me to have sympathy for people like that. I understand mental illness or depression, but some people have to pull themselves up by their own bootstraps and overcome obstacles instead of letting things defeat them.

Growing up and living my life, I've found out that my best friend is me. Of course, this is before I had a wife and child, but back then, it was just me. I know me. I know what I like and what I don't like. I try to do what's best for me. I've never robbed from anybody or stole from any-body, especially me.

It's an issue of trust, and I have learned throughout my life that the only person I can really, really trust is me. Because I know me. I talk to me every day. I've been with me longer than anybody. I was an only child and had all these imaginary friends and games I would play. And I lived in a hotel with 104 apartments. Most people who lived there were single or were married and didn't have any kids. At most, there were three or four kids in the building. The way I looked at it is I had 170 people to mess with, look at their lives, and just watch everything.

You have to be your own best friend. I will never, ever do anything to hurt me. I trust me completely. My children may hurt me, and my wife may divorce me. But I will never hurt me, and anyone reading this should know that too. I live inside of this 180-pound, six-foot shell. I can look out and no one can look in. I'm always aware of everything around me. And if you can't count on yourself to back you up, how can you count on anyone else?

I was walking down the street one night in New York. I had a bad cold and went to the Carnegie Deli that a friend of mine owned. It was a long walk, but I was willing to do it because all I wanted was some good, old-fashioned chicken soup. I made my way there and had a great bowl of soup. I felt a little better. When I was walking back, I saw some rough-looking guys on the street. I crossed the street to avoid them. As I did that, I recalled that someone told me a long time ago that if you act nuts on the streets of New York or anywhere for that matter, no one would dare mess with you. In fact, if I ever got held up, I'd throw up on my money. I don't think any mugger would be too interested in taking it.

So, I thought I knew what those rough-looking guys were thinking. "That guy is by himself and has bleached blonde hair." I figured trouble was coming my way and there was nothing I could do about it. Here comes the chair. I had to act like I was nuts. I had no other choice. I saw the shadow moving in, so I immediately started doing all this Jackie Chan-Kung Fu stuff. "Hi ya. Ha. Ha. Ha," I yelled. I turned around quickly and there was no one there. It was the shadow from the streetlight. That's right. Jackie "The Brain" Chan was scared of his own shadow, grasshopper.

A lack of trust is a chair shot that doesn't stop. Some guys in wrestling just wouldn't trust you. I was working against the Big Bossman, taking the place of Rick Rude because he hurt his arm. I only had to go a couple of minutes with Bossman. He's six foot five and 300 pounds. There was no way I could have a match with the guy and make it look like I could beat him in any way, shape, or form. That didn't matter and wasn't even the point of that match. People wanted to see me get beat. My goal was to entertain people as it always has been.

Bossman carried this nightstick to the ring with him. I decided to walk into the ring with a Hulk Hogan Wrestling Buddy for him to give to his mother. At the time, my angle with him was that I was saying all these derogatory things about her and wanted to give her a wrestling buddy to make things right. My plan was that I was going to back into the corner and kiss his ass. But I wanted him to focus on the doll. That way, I could poke him in the eyes so he'd drop the nightstick. I would get a shot in with the nightstick and then throw him to the ropes. He'd come off and when I went to go for a clothesline, he'd duck. I would get nailed by him and throw the nightstick in the air. He'd catch it, and I was all his.

When I told Bossman of the idea, he wouldn't do it. He said, "That's my gimmick. You can't have my nightstick."

He didn't trust me. Some guys wouldn't trust you because they thought you'd just beat on them and make them look weak and I can understand that. But I was giving Bossman 90 percent of the match if not more and establishing a good comeback for him. I wanted to get some heat on him. He would get that "gimmick" back, get his hand raised in victory, and get paid for the night's work. Bottom line.

I liked him then, and I still like him. He's a real nice guy, but he was a little green at the time. I was not out to screw him. I was just out to make money with him. But he didn't trust me and grazed my head with that chair.

Maybe I learned that truthfulness is not always the best way to go about things. I have lied, but who hasn't? Sometimes I think kids, including me when I was growing up, are raised to lie. In life, you're told to tell Aunt Edna that her tuna casserole is delicious, even though the old bag is trying to poison you with that garbage. We're teaching kids to act like "heels" at a very early age. Obviously, you don't want to hurt Aunt Edna's feelings, but there is nothing worse than a bad batch of tuna casserole.

We all lie, and in that sense, we all deliver our own chair shots. It's the way life is. I won't and no one should lie about things that will hurt people worse than metal hitting your skull. I'll lie about having a reservation for dinner. "We don't see it here," they say. "Well, I called." I won't lie about anything that will cost anyone money, harm their position in life, or just do harm in general. There are things in life I know I have to do to make it easier for me. Because if I don't, those people out there aren't going to do it for me. If they liked me, really liked me, they would pay my mortgage. And they don't. I was never promised anything. I wouldn't get what I expected. I was treated badly by some that I really idolized.

Pat O'Connor gave me great advice—"Learn to work." That goes for the ring, the dressing room, the promoter's office, and the television studios of both professional wrestling and life. Sometimes, you unfortunately can't avoid a chair shot and have to block it with one of your own. However you get your income and wherever your money is coming from, learn to work with those people who control it. Because, I guarantee you, they're either working with you or just working you with a chair in hand.

People worry about the right look, about what they are wearing and nothing else. I never worried about wearing a tuxedo to the ring, because I would need seven of them, one for every day of the week. Ever try to find a dry cleaner who would clean mud, manure, blood, and anything else you could imagine out of a tux on a rush basis? I chose sweat suits with sequins on them. Wearing sunglasses was silly, because no one could see my eyes and I could lose an eye if they got broken while I was wearing them. I never carried anything to the ring with me, like a cane, because that took up one hand.

My point is that people have to worry about how they're performing and doing their job in any walk of life. I'd do business with a guy who was working out of his trailer as opposed to a Beverly Hills office suite, just as long as he was honest. I've been in those fancy offices with a lot of agents. They talk a lot of stuff and most of it never happens. The rent is probably $10,000 a month, but if they're not honest, I can't deal with them. I can't trust them. And there's probably a lot of metal folding chairs around.

I don't really even care if someone does something wrong to me. I just want to be told and have that person be honest with me. Hell, I've done 14 things wrong today, but if I told you, I'd have to kill you.

That is how I approached doing this book and the one before this. Tell the truth. That's either the best way to guard against chair shots, or the best way to get them. A lot of people in the wrestling business never wanted to tell the truth. A lot of them wrote books and told their stories as if wrestling was real. Some guys still want to make it look real, because it makes them look good. They don't realize that people respect us more for our acting and performing abilities than our fighting abilities.

People don't believe it's real for the most part, and if you try to tell them it is real, you'll just insult them.

I think the easiest way to get through a chair shot—no matter what kind it is and no matter if you deserve it or not—is to just take it head on. If you have to go to court, go. If your spouse is going to leave you for someone else, shake the hand of the person taking him or her and thank them for saving you the time and money you would have continued to waste on that person. It could have gone on much, much longer.

Make the best out of chair shots. Take them, but don't sell them. Don't let people see you weak or defenseless. Here's my advice. The next time you get hit in the head with a chair shot and they crush your noggin with that metal, opening you up with a huge cut, just smile and say, "The blood feels fine." Be better than them by taking it better than they could ever give it.

Or better yet, look them straight in the eye and say, "Smell my head."

CHAPTER 7

Role Models

Y ou have to look back and laugh at things. My mother and I often saw how silly we could be.

For some reason, my mother could never match colors together. I had to take her to the hospital one day. She decided to wear a pair of socks with polka dots on them with a green dress. On top of that, she had red hair with a striped babushka covering part of it. This man walked by her who was about 70. He had plaid pair of pants on and a jacket that didn't match. She had the nerve to nudge me, point at him, and say, "Get him."

I told her, "Hey, what are you laughing at? You look like Ronald McDonald's mom."

She laughed and I laughed.

When I was a kid growing up, I didn't have a father. My dad left my mother, and who knows why he did that. I'm not really sure why and, frankly, it's not important to me. She may have been a pain in the butt. He may have been a pain in the butt. On top of that, if they had stayed together, I wonder how it would have affected me. I'll never understand why people claim that they stayed together because of their kids. Some feel that both parents have to be around, no matter how miserable they make each other and how it affects their kids.

I was never affected because I had everything I needed from my mother. My dad was gone, and he did what he had to do. I told him that when I first saw his grave a few years ago. I'm not mad at him. I'm not

"If you're poor and you do something stupid, you're nuts. If you're rich and do something stupid, you're eccentric."

mad at my mother. I never felt mad and never felt cheated by him not being there. At "father and son" days at school, I just didn't go. At one point, I thought my dad had died. When I'd ask my mom about that, she would just say that he was gone. There were never pictures of my father or any evidence that he even existed. He was just gone.

I had so much love from my mother, grandmother, aunt, and friends, I just never missed him, because my life was filled with family. I was never raised with him. If I was and he was loving and caring and then left, I would have felt that loss. It never bothered me because I didn't know him and so I didn't know the difference when he was gone. He could never hurt me or make me sad, because we never interacted with each other. Plus, I was too busy sabotaging the neighbor's grill or stirring up some kind of trouble. My mother never even said he was a bad person. They just didn't get along. He didn't miss me playing high school football and baseball games, because I didn't do that kind of thing. I only went to grade school. The only activity I ever participated in was Little League, and my mom and grandma would come to see me.

There was so much love in my home, I wasn't interested in finding him until several years ago. I didn't want a relationship with him and I honestly didn't think he was even alive. I just wanted to see a picture of him to see if I looked like him. It turned out to be immensely rewarding when I found my brothers. From what I could gather, the old man wouldn't have been a bad guy. He probably would have spanked me for all the trouble I got myself into. He raised my three brothers who turned out to be real decent people, so he had to have done something right.

Or he moved out on them, too. I'm not sure.

From what I understand, he was a strict Irish Catholic. He liked to have a little "taste" now and then. He was a printer and worked at a railroad and in a bar. If a guy came into the bar with nothing, my dad would give him a suit and he would walk home in the bum's clothes. He used to wear cymbals on his knees and played a broomstick to entertain people. How about that? He never stole anything or conned anybody. He just sang and told jokes.

I was told he was a very honest man. He loved baseball and he loved the ladies just a little more. I'm told by a lot of people in the family that I'm just like him.

People sometimes blame the way their life has gone and they point to not having a father figure. I think that whoever raised them—father, mother, or anyone—didn't raise them right. Let's say that a man and woman have a boy. The father beats his kid and beats his wife while the kid is sitting there. The kid is watching the whole thing. In those situations, the kids judge their father, and the mother probably knocks him while he sits in jail. If you don't think that affects a kid, you're crazy.

My mom didn't really play the "father figure." Then again, I don't even know what that is. I never really saw my friends' dads, as they would come home at 6:00 and stay in their apartments. On Saturday and Sunday, we played ball, walked to the Cubs game, and hung out at the beach. In those days, kids were "seen and not heard." You never heard a dad yell, "Hey Tom, throw the ball to me," primarily because there was no place to throw a ball. It was an apartment complex.

Not having a father never came into play. I never saw my friends cry because their dad was gone or bad to them. Never, ever did that come into the picture. I think that you should appreciate the parent or parents you have, whether it's a mom, dad, or someone else. And don't create a problem or conflict in your life because you don't have something that others already have.

My mother dated from time to time. She had a boyfriend I resented, but only because he was taking attention away from me. It had nothing to do with my dad or if I thought she was betraying him or me. I just didn't like the guy.

When they were dating, they would often go out for the night. I didn't want my mom to go out, and I was going to do everything I could to make sure she stayed home. I knew where he parked his car, so I would walk outside after he came to the hotel to pick her up. I took a knife and cut the valves off his tires. As I walked back to the hotel, I saw them leaving in a cab.

They double-crossed me and didn't "sell" the tire slashing.

This "friend" of my mom was with us once when my aunt was going to go back to Indianapolis. We all walked her out of the hotel.

"Where are you going?" he asked me.

"I'm going with my aunt to the train station," I said. "She told me I could go."

"No you're not," he said and then he pie-faced me, pushing me to the ground.

At 14 years old, I jumped on this bastard and knocked him down. My aunt started to scream. I started yelling at him, "This is my aunt. This is my mother. Who are you to tell me anything?"

My mother dumped him after that. She didn't want anyone telling me what I could do and couldn't do.

She only dated one other guy that I knew of. This other guy would come over to the house with a six-pack of beer. My grandmother (did I tell you she was like Schultz from *Hogan's Heroes*?) would sit with them the whole time, folding her arms. At 10:00, she would glare at the guy and say, "Don't you have something to do?"

How many guys do you think would come back after that? That guy never did.

I guess my mother was a great example to me because she had a sense of humor. I think that's important in life, and I think I have a sense of humor because of her. We would both watch people and see how silly some people could be.

We both got a kick how people spoke in our neighborhood in Chicago. They would talk so funny and put their words completely out of place. For example, they would be standing by the street with a baby in their arms. Instead of asking, "Throw the baby's hat out the window," they would say, "Throw the baby out the window its hat." Instead of saying, "Throw the baby's buggy down the stairs," they would say, "Throw the baby down the stairs its buggy." Honestly, that's the way they talked. If the person they were shouting to only caught the first part of the sentence, there would be trouble.

For me, the term role model applies not only to someone who teaches you how to be as a person, but also to someone who teaches you how not to be based on the example they set. I had an uncle named Johnny who was more like "The Brain" than anyone I've ever known. He was my grandfather's brother and worked for him in his store from time to time. Johnny was a complete scam artist and just flimflammed around. He was the kind of guy who would sell people very expensive "Oriental Chow Dogs," but what he would do is get a big furry dog that he found on the street and clip all of its hair and half the tail so it would look really odd. The "Oriental Chow Dog" was usually just a poodle with a lousy haircut.

Johnny would even hand paint on rugs he bought or stole from the store and sell them as imported Oriental hand-painted rugs. People would even buy them, walk on them, and get paint on their shoes. He couldn't wait to sell them and would often unload them before the paint was dry.

When his kids needed shoes, he would go to my grandfather and ask for money. Keep in mind, he always had tailored suits, a white shirt and tie, white gloves, and a Humburg like Eisenhower had. He'd bring his daughters with him when he asked for help, just for sympathy. My grandfather would always give him a check, not being able to turn down his nieces. Johnny would go to the store and make out the check for $20 when both pairs of shoes would only cost five dollars and kept the $15 dollars for himself.

He met some women and had them sign over everything to him. He left his wife and family, and they didn't find him until five years later in Michigan. He had gone through all of some woman's money. But that's what he would do, just disappear for years at a time. He was able to get to women because he was very handsome, suave, and boy could he talk.

A woman walked into my grandfather's store to return a robe she had purchased earlier. My grandfather believed that the customer was always right, so he took the robe to the back and figured out how much it cost. He went to the cash register and took out $10. The woman said, "No, I paid $30 for it."

"You paid 30? Who did you buy it from?"

"It was a tall man with white gloves."

My uncle Johnny.

Another job that Johnny had with my grandfather was traveling around with a steamer trunk full of samples to show to clothing stores. In those days, people would travel with these big trunks where you could open them up and there would be places where you could hang your clothes. My grandfather gave Johnny this trunk and the samples.

One day, someone from the Schroeder Hotel in Milwaukee called my grandfather in Chicago. The guy from the hotel asked, "Do you know a Johnny Trembacz?"

My grandfather said, "Yes I do."

"Well, he hasn't paid his room bill here for quite some time, so we confiscated his trunk."

My grandfather thought to himself, "My God, he's going to take all those suits. What's Johnny done now?"

He traveled to Milwaukee, which must have taken him forever. I don't know how fast he could have gone from Chicago to Milwaukee because there were no interstates in the '20s. He got to the hotel, paid the bill that Johnny owed, and claimed the trunk. He opened it up to find it filled with rocks. Johnny had taken all the suits.

When my grandfather died, the family—my mother, her sister, her brother, and their grandmother—asked Johnny if he'd run the business because they knew nothing about it. He had at least worked there, even if he wasn't familiar with the pricing policies. It was funny, because he said, "Oh no, I can't steal from you people."

In thinking about Johnny, I realized that he had never come to mind before when I was developing my wrestling character. I had not thought of him until I was working on this book. No one knew whatever became of him. He vanished in the '30s, and no one ever saw him again.

Maybe I have a different take than most people when it comes to family, but remember, blood is not thicker than water.

Scotch is.

Blood is blood. It travels through your veins and it can link you biologically to other people. But it doesn't mean you have an emotional attachment to them. It doesn't mean that you must look at them as role models. Sometimes, a family may not have one role model among them. If you're looking for someone to have an influence on you, you can find someone outside of your family.

Vince McMahon was a great role model when it came to work ethic. Someone you knew would listen to you. He always told me that I could call him anytime, day or night, if there was a problem or something wasn't right. If I had an idea in the middle of the night—2, 3, 4, or 5 in the morning—he didn't care. And when I would give him an idea, he would always say, "I'm going to put it into the computer," or, "That's been done," not "That's the dumbest thing that I've ever heard," or, "That won't work. What are you, stupid?" Whether he felt that or not, I'll never know. He listened, which everyone should do.

Vince is firm but fair. I missed a show once because I was in Gorilla Monsoon's daughter's wedding. That night, I had to be in St. Louis, working a cage match with Hulk Hogan and Paul Orndorff. But there I was with Monsoon and his family and a lot of old-time wrestlers. I was having such a good time, but there was a 1:00 plane that would have gotten me into St. Louis at 3:00 or 4:00 in the afternoon. Another one left at 4:00 or 5:00. I figured that I didn't have to be at the building until 9:00, so I was covered there. I chose the later flight, but then it ended up getting cancelled. There was no other way to get to St. Louis, so I went home.

Vince called me the next day. "Where were you?" he asked. I told him the truth about what happened and my decision-making process. "Well, I have to fine you. You realize that, don't you?"

I started giving him all these reasons and excuses.

"No, no, no. You're not listening to me. You're trying to think of an answer. I'm telling you that you missed St. Louis. You were on top and in the main event. I'm going to have to fine you. Blackjack Lanza, the agent and your old partner, will fine you."

I agreed with him. Jack and I always had a relationship where if he had control and had to do something authoritative, he did it. He was straight up with you if you broke the rules. I never took advantage of our friendship whether I didn't show up, showed up late, or wanted to leave early. Business is business.

If you do take advantage of a situation and say, "Hey, I thought we were friends," then you never were a good friend in the first place. It's hard to mix business and friendship. Many times, it creates hard feelings and a friendship is sometimes destroyed. Mutual respect for that person and what he or she does in a position of authority will prevent that from happening. In that situation, Jack was a great role model, because he was able to separate the two. Yes, I was going to be out some money, but Jack had a job to do.

Jack fined me $500 bucks for missing the show. When I got to the next town, Jack told me that he talked to Vince, and he didn't think the fine was enough. He had to fine me another $500.

He looked me in the eye and said, "Do you understand?" I said, "Yes, I certainly do." We shook hands and changed the subject.

Choose your role models carefully. Learn from what they do and what they don't do. There's an old saying about keeping friends close and enemies closer. The exception would be my Uncle Johnny. Keep a guy like him the closest of all, but don't let him within reach of your wallet.

CHAPTER 8

Education or
Life Experiences

I noticed that there are a lot of things in life that are very peculiar. The secret, I've found, is to sit back and watch these things, and that's how you're going to learn. In school, I knew when I was standing on my toes trying to reach the urinal that the Boston Tea Party wouldn't affect my life. I didn't care who Magellan was. I didn't care about the Santa Maria and the Pinto, but I used to own a Pinto. I knew I'd never use it. I just wanted to watch wrestling and television overall. There were things being taught to me that I'd never use, but I'd use everything that I'd seen through life just happening in front of me one way or another.

Had there been no wrestling for me and I had never had the opportunity to see it live or in person, I still don't know if I would have finished school beyond my eighth grade education. I don't know if I would have gone any further. I had to quit more because of my family than any love for professional wrestling, but I'm not sure what I would have done. I'd have maybe been a bartender or the guy who oiled down the nudie girls at a strip club. Maybe I would have become a radio talk show host. I wanted to be a disk jockey at one point, but I realized that I couldn't talk and read at the same time.

"For those of you who dropped out of high school, remember the famous phrase, 'Do you want fries with that?'"

Education is key to life and everyone needs it, because that will lead to the kind of job that provides profit sharing and insurance. While it's not a guarantee, you can certainly increase your chances of having those luxuries in life. When I was a kid taking bumps and flying all over the place, I never thought I'd get hurt. My arm didn't feel good sometimes or my back was sore after a match. When I got older, I got cancer. My wife got cancer twice. All the bills started coming. It taught me that it's smart to have some damn good insurance and think ahead about that stuff.

If I wanted to get a job right now outside of professional wrestling, I couldn't. I'm 59 years old, and who's going to hire a 59-year-old guy with cancer? I can't drive a car because I have trouble turning my head to the right due to neck injuries. I have atrophy in my right hand, so I can't do physical work or pick up stuff. My knees are bad and my ankles are shot. There's nothing I can do.

I guess I'm kind of like a pet at home. A 180-pound housecat. I'm housebroke, but I still spray the curtains. I know how to find the porcelain chair. I like to go outside because of the nice breeze. Not in the daytime though, because the squirrels are out. I enjoy the sun and I enjoy Florida. I don't have many hobbies, but I have my friends and we all love to laugh. But as far as a job, no one is going to hire me. I can't get benefits at 59 with cancer. Physically, I can't do anything. I have a seventh grade education. I don't know computers. The only thing I can do is write this book that some of you won't even pay for and just borrow it from your friends.

You deadbeats.

If I could go back and get an education, I would have liked to know more about computers and how to use them. I could take classes and learn, but I'm too old and set in my ways. I don't think that I can be educated any more. It sounds silly and I know people go to college at the age of 70, but I just don't have that retention or an attention span anymore. I've been kicked in the head too many times, and don't forget that my head smells like ass.

I wish I learned more in school and read more books. But in a way, my life experiences made up for anything I missed by not getting a formal education. I traveled all over the world. I got to meet very important people. Vince McMahon had a bunch of wrestlers at a table for a banquet honoring Dick Enberg and Phil Rizzuto at the Marriott in New York. President George Bush was supposed to be speaking there, but it was during the Persian Gulf War and for security reasons, he couldn't make it. So they brought in vice president Dan Quayle—who is also a native of Indiana. I started wrestling in Indiana, for those people who don't know or who are bumming this book.

I introduced myself to him. He said, "Oh yeah, I remember you. I used to see Dick the Bruiser kick your butt all the time."

I said, "Yeah, I think I'll vote Democrat next time around."

I am friends with George Steinbrenner, who owns the Yankees; Dick Ebersol, who is president of NBC Sports; George Schlatter, who produced *Laugh-In* and *Real People* and worked with Muhammad Ali and Frank Sinatra; and Soupy Sales. I know a lot of people, from Presidents to the bluest of blue collars. I know every form of life. I would have never had that if I had worried about the Boston Tea Party. I was lucky enough to educate myself and be open to be educated on what was out there. That's the key, whether you're sitting in a classroom or on an airplane going to a new place. Open your mind. Open your brain.

I don't think school was meant for me, anyway. When I was a kid, I got expelled from public school because of my attendance record. My mother had three choices. One was this detention school for really bad kids—kind of like daycare in San Quentin. She didn't want me to go there, and I didn't either. The other two options were a Catholic school or a Protestant school. I couldn't get into those because I needed to have my father sign for me, and no one knew where he was.

So my mother made a huge sacrifice and sent me to a private school for $65 a month. The "teacher" was a retired major from a military academy and he ran the place out of his house. He had a glass eye with a flag on it. He'd roll his eye until the flag came up. It felt like I was being taught by a slot machine. Everyone in his class were criminals, mentally challenged kids, or problem kids like me. He'd always have us read a book and he'd leave the room.

If you were bad, he'd send you into another room to be by yourself as punishment. But this room had a radio, a window open, and a *Life* magazine. He would make you stay in there all day, and you didn't have to be in the "classroom" with the criminals and the retards. That taught me to intentionally screw up, and I did. He would smack me with a ruler right across the wrist. "Come on, Raymond," he'd say, leading me to the room. "You have to stay here." So, I took one across the wrist on purpose, but all day long, I could look out the window, read the magazine, and listen to the radio. As long as my mom paid the 65 bucks a month, I couldn't flunk.

I never quite knew why we were there in the first place. At lunchtime, they put us in a big hall. The major would take us over to Lincoln Park from noon until two. We'd go back to the "school" until three. You could stay overnight if you wanted to. It was like a work release program at a prison. Actually, it was a gimmick for that human slot machine to make money.

When winter would come—and this is how I started self-educating myself—I would ask him if I could shovel his walk. What I ended up doing was shoveling everyone else's sidewalks too, including the cleaners and the drugstore down the street. Everyone gave me a buck for doing it. I made five bucks, came back at three, put the shovel in the back, and went home.

The major had no idea. I made five bucks a day shoveling snow, eating lunch, reading a book and a *Life* magazine, and getting by a ruler. I passed. Hell, I could have been valedictorian. Who said that I wasn't getting an education?

In the end, that was the last school I went to. I never graduated and never came back the last couple of weeks. We moved to Indianapolis, and I needed to work to support my mother, aunt, and grandmother.

I never learned anything at that school. I didn't learn anything in the seven or so years I was in school. I ended up learning more in the wrestling business, riding in cars and listening to guys talk. Watching people wait on me in stores and serving me in restaurants and even people who handle your business is a great lesson in human behavior. That's where you learn things.

Now while I wasn't learning anything in school, my decision to leave was based more upon my family needs than my desire to goof around and watch television. My mom made the decision to move to Indianapolis to stay at my aunt's house and take care of her. My aunt was suffering from breast cancer. My mom sacrificed her job managing the apartment building in Chicago. It allowed us to stay in the biggest apartment in the building with our rent and utilities paid for. On top of that, she made 50 bucks a week, but quit to take care of her sister.

Her sacrifice led to my sacrifice. I left the classroom to enter the school of hard knocks. It would teach me lessons about how to live life, deal with people, and, many years later, fight my own battle with cancer. I allowed these experiences in my life to educate me. You have to keep yourself open to learn, no matter if it's a teacher in front of a classroom or my very sick aunt and my mother dedicated to care for her.

My aunt suffered so much during her battle with cancer. They didn't have the medicine back in 1960 that they do now. Her one breast was the size of a football and it was all blue with lines on it. She had a mastectomy and radiation, which made her whole side seem burned like a turkey. At the age of 15, I had to give her constant shots of Demerol in her butt because neither my mother, grandmother, nor my aunt could do it. My grandmother was too old and my mother was too nervous. She would try to push the needle in instead of popping it in. I filled the needle, gave my aunt the shot, disinfected the area with alcohol, and put a Band-Aid over it. Every day, she would need a new shot.

I never felt bad about doing those types of things at such a young age or even having to work to support them. I was never miserable about missing out on other things that people of my age were experiencing and enjoying. In fact, I was happy. I was able to keep my aunt alive for a little longer because of what I could do for her. Besides, it was more fun going to work than going to school, because I was doing something for a change. I was contributing and I was making other people happy. I wasn't in school getting a formal education, but I was still learning and earning my way.

With my mother having to take care of her sister, and my grandmother being too old to go get a job, I was the only able-bodied worker in the house. I certainly didn't want my mom working on the side with everything she would have to do for my aunt. She tried that. She took a job for a short time with a cleaner. One day, I walked by and saw her bent over, throwing people's dirty clothes into a bag and trying to carry it across the room. She couldn't even lift it and had to drag it. I couldn't take it.

I walked into the store and stood her up. I said, "Go home. I'll finish up today."

"You can't do that," she said.

"Go home."

I sent her home and finished up her work. I had no idea what I was doing. The manager walked in and said, "Who are you?"

I said, "I'm Millie's son. She no longer works here. She's not feeling well."

I left the cleaners on that day and decided that my mother would never put somebody's dirty underwear in a bag when I was perfectly able to do it. It bugged me to see it, and it was something I never wanted to see again.

For my efforts in working, I always got a check every week. And I did what I had to do to get a check. Whenever I filled out an application, I would check "yes" for the question about being a high school graduate. My mother asked me, "Why do you do that? It's lying."

"But, mom," I explained to her. "By the time they find out I'm not a high school grad, I may have three or four checks. And if I'm doing a good job, they may keep me."

Back in the '60s, there were no computers that could check that information. I always had a job someplace. I could always find work. Even if they found out, I could get a job someplace else. I'm not saying it was the right thing to do, but again, it was about sacrificing. Maybe lying on an application takes a little bit of integrity away from me, but I still kept food on the table and a roof over their heads. And I was determined to prove that I didn't need the degree to get the job done. My education was outside of school, and it wouldn't stop after high school or college.

So, I just did it with no resentment whatsoever. Had I got a regular job my whole life, I wouldn't have made the money I made in wrestling. And I wouldn't have gotten to see Chris Taylor naked. I wouldn't have gotten choked out by Mad Dog Vachon.

I've never thought I was having a bad life. I've had a great life. There were some things I didn't like about it, but overall, I'm happy how things have turned out and wouldn't change my childhood for anything.

I think education is important, but I think some people with influence don't feel the same way. If education is so valued in society, why aren't teachers paid more? They should get bigger checks, not the guy with the bald head and the underwear who puts a ball in a hoop. Teaching requires dedication, because chances are they're not going to be millionaires. If you choose to be a teacher and take a minimum salary, there are two reasons. Either you're really for the kids or you're as dumb as a mud finch and wasting your and the kids' time.

While school wasn't for me, people have to get that education nowadays. Get that diploma. Get that sheepskin. Not the one with the hole in it like I have from the wrong end of the sheep. You need a bachelor's degree to really make any money at all.

My degree is the aches and pains I feel from years of bumping in the ring. My degree is the experiences I've had and the anecdotes I tell. My degree is that my family has been able to live a good life because I worked and learned at the very same time.

CHAPTER 9

Big Payoffs,
Good News and Bad News

I was driving from Indianapolis to Detroit with Baron Von Raschke, about a 300-mile trip. In Jackson, Michigan, there is a state penitentiary that we passed by all the time. I told the Baron, "Jim, you know those guys make seven cents a day in there."

Baron said, "Wait a minute, Heenan. Is this another one of your 'get rich quick' schemes?"

You want to follow a dream and make a little money? Boy, I don't know about professional wrestling. There's money in it, but only if you're a star. But it takes forever to become a star in anything. It takes forever to make a lot of money. Making money is no secret. It's just like staying alive in this world.

There's a saying in our business. "It's not how much you make, it's how much you save."

Not that making money wasn't tricky sometimes. They had weird ways of paying you when you worked in various territories, and you were never reimbursed for travel. Some promoters would pay you in fives after the match. They'd be counting it out by fives. Five, 10, 15, 20, and so on. The minute they saw you smile at the money you had in your hand, they would stop.

"Some people are so dumb, they can hide their own Easter Eggs."

One trip, I drove from Indianapolis to work in St. Louis. After St. Louis, Moose Morowski—that's a good name for a wrestler; you can tell he's not a fashion designer—and I drove back to Kansas City. I drove 500 miles that day. That's where a lot of misconceptions were made about what a professional wrestler earns. The average guy thinks we're in the ring for about 10 minutes, just fake wrestling and making millions of dollars. Not me. After 500 miles, I probably made $125.

We got up on Saturday morning and drove to Topeka to do television. I made 10 dollars and had the rest of the day off. That night, we drove to St. Joseph to do television at 10:00 in the evening. Gus Karas, the promoter, always had a hat that matched his suit and shoes. If he wore a green hat, you could count on him wearing a green suit and shoes. He would give out these big watches, and the face of it would always be cockeyed. You could always tell if someone worked for Gus in St. Joe if they were wearing that watch.

He normally paid five dollars for television. No, that wasn't a typo. He paid five bucks after the hundreds of miles that I traveled. After we were done, Gus walked up to me at 11:00 at night, handed me 10 bucks, and said, "Bobby, do you have a five on you?"

That's right. I didn't even have a chance to smile. I was getting one five and that was it.

I said, "It's in my wallet. I'll be right back."

I went out to my car, got in, and drove 500 miles back home to Indianapolis. That's where my wallet was.

As I drove away, I remembered Tor Kamata telling me once not to drive the Interstate when I drove to Indianapolis. "Go on Highway 36," he said. "It's faster and there are no cops."

He was absolutely right. But there are no gas stations either. Thank God I had that 10 on me.

I got home at seven in the morning and my mom said, "I thought you were going to be gone for a week."

"I made 20 bucks, mom. And I drove 1,000 miles."

But for the most part it was a good life, and a lot of guys lived it up by spending their money. I knew guys like Dr. Jerry Graham back in the late '50s and early '60s. He'd walk down the street, lighting his cigars with hundred dollar bills. Well, that was impressive to a lot of people who never had a hundred bucks in their life. But if you have a hundred bucks, you know how stupid that is. But that's the way he was and that's the way a lot of guys were. Money was easy to come by for them. Graham was probably making $100,000 a year.

I would see these wrestlers who would walk into the bar and buy drinks for everyone in the house. They wore $20,000 Rolexes with their

Mercedes parked out front. Some guys never realized that the checks and the big payoffs were going to come to an end someday. That goes for anybody. And when that check does stop coming, you're never going to recoup that money you gave away to everyone else. Your earning power stops after a certain time. That $20,000 Rolex you're wearing is worth much more now, if you buy it new. Same with those diamond rings and gold chains.

I had the honor of meeting Joe Louis many years ago towards the end of his career. He had just received his payoff in cash and told the person standing next to him, "This is the most money I've hand in my hand at one time." Think about that. How many people must have taken his money? I wonder if he ever got his money. Just like Mike Tyson and Don King fighting over the money they made. If Louis or Tyson got $20 million to fight for one night, they never saw a check for $20 million that night. By the time they would pay for the entourage and the top floor at Caesar's, not to mention paying the manager and the IRS, there's not that much left.

That's a shame. A pitiful shame.

Everybody always bitches about athletes and all the money they make. Even I wonder about it sometimes. Anybody reading this book, including any deadbeat who bummed this book off someone else, needs to think about it. If they gave you $10 million to hit a round ball with a bat at 20 years of age, would you take it? Would you get in your boxer shorts and bounce a ball into a basket? Would you put on pads and a helmet and run like hell so no one catches you? Of course you would. They're not making too much money. The owners are giving them too much. Society accepts it and others who work harder and contribute more to this world get literally shortchanged. And then everyone yells about the athletes being a bunch of spoiled brats. Well, someone else is doing the spoiling.

You know what I'd be doing if I had had $20 million at 20 years old? I'd be doing time right now in San Quentin. I guarantee it. Thank God those guys have agents. They're the ones who make the deals, because those kids don't know any better. All they know is someone is willing to pay them a ton of money.

It's like Vince McMahon paying himself a $1 million salary and performance bonuses when business is down. Guess what, it's his money. And if Hulk Hogan left WWE in 2003 because of his payoff, that makes him a smart businessman. The only way to be successful in this business is to look out for yourself. Let's face it, Hulk's only been in one business. He's never owned a wrestling company. Everything he made is because of Hulk Hogan and because of this business. In my opinion, he was the greatest star we ever had. He wrote the foreword for my first book, and I have nothing but good things to say about him, so I may be biased in that respect.

The money Hogan made from this business that no one else has ever made is wonderful. If someone wasn't paying him right or something was wrong with his payoff, he's smart enough to know what many don't even think about. Promoters don't put on a show to make people happy or to make the wrestlers money. How many people do you know who put on any kind of show, whether it's wrestling, Las Vegas, or a movie, and say, "We're going to put in $100 million, and I hope we break even so the talent makes money and the people watching it leave happy." Vince paying himself at the so-called expense of his talent is life. Hogan leaving the WWF over money is life.

How many people are selling a cooker on television that can bake a moose in a half-hour? You think they want you to eat good moose? They want to make money. You can't do anything in this world without money, so that's what it's all about: getting the payoff.

I've seen guys in this business who were in the main event one week and the following week they weren't. The week they were the main eventer the house would do $10,000. When someone else was in their spot, they would want the house to do $9,000 or less. I always wanted the house to do $12,000 or $15,000. I figured I would get paid more based on how many people were there rather than where I was on the card. Sometimes you were on salary, but sometimes they would throw you a bone of 30 or 50 bucks if things were hot. That small gesture meant a lot to me.

People I knew in the business were both glory- and money-hungry. A promoter would bring someone into their promotion and give them $1,000 a week and make them the champion. Or they'd bring a guy in, not use him all that well, and not make him the champion. But they would make $1,500 a week. Some wrestlers would refuse that and would not come into that territory. They wanted to be the champion, regardless of money. Gorilla Monsoon would call them fools.

I've never had fans walk up to the ring and say, "Good bump," or, "Good backdrop," and give me five bucks. Hell, I tip people who bring me food that they're supposed to bring me. I give money to the mailman on Christmas to do the job he's supposed to do. A football player will score a touchdown and spike it. That's what his job is, to score touchdowns. You don't see the mailman high-fiving everyone because he got the letter in the box. That's his job. Wrestling was my job, and no one ever tipped me.

Some guys live this business 24 hours a day and they constantly gripe about the payoffs and the travel. If they're reading this, my advice to them is get another job. Go do something for yourself. If you don't like the business, then quit. There's a saying in our business, if you're looking for sympathy, you'll find it in the dictionary.

Between shit and syphilis.

Had I not invested my money and saved it along with my wife, I don't know what I'd be doing. It wasn't a conscious decision that I was going to save my money when I started in the business. I'm not sure it ever is when you first start. Whenever my money came in, I spent it on my mom and my grandma. The rest I spent on myself and had a ball.

As I got more successful, I would have $2,500 to $3,000 a month in American Express charges just in bar tabs. Ray Stevens and I would go in and not buy the house a drink, but buy the other boys a round. Sometimes, it's 10 guys and you're buying more rounds. It turns into a lot of money when you do that five to six times a week. I never made that kind of money before, and it was fun to have it and spend it.

With the minimal education I had, I wouldn't have known about investing had someone not helped me. I talked to a financial advisor who asked me if I had money to waste. I said, "No." He told me not to invest in the stock market because it's like gambling. Unless you can afford to lose it, don't "bet." He was right. It wasn't until I got married and had a kid that I started saving my money. My wife Cindi made some good investments, with the "Ks" and the mutual funds. And I can live until Thursday if she doesn't want to eat or have electricity.

I didn't see the value of saving my money or any examples of people who did or didn't save their money when I broke into the business. I was just in awe of the business. As I got older, I saw guys who shouldn't have been in the ring anymore and shouldn't have been driving in the towns. They just shouldn't have been active wrestlers anymore. Their motivation was to get the payoff.

Some wrestlers lost a lot of money investing in the bar business. Someone would approach a wrestler and say, "I want to open a bar with you." I never wanted to get into that business, because it's like the wrestling business. It's money coming in that I can't control. Someone else would see it before I would, because I would be out on the road and not there every day. Someone else would touch it and make it disappear. Plus, it's a lot of hours if you are there.

Joe Tangaro was a good friend of mine who wrestled as Joe Bernetti with Guy Bernetti as the Bernetti brothers. He was a wonderful guy and gave me the best advice I ever got. He said, "Don't let the Bruiser make you into an errand boy. Be a man."

Joe owned a successful steakhouse in St. Louis. I was very proud of him and told him so one day when I paid him a visit. I said, "This is great. You have a restaurant. You no longer have to drive a car or fly."

"This is the worst thing I've ever done," he said. "If the dishwasher doesn't show up, I have to wash dishes. If the parking lot guy doesn't show up, I have to park cars. I have to be here every minute of every day, seven days a week. I didn't realize any of that."

It's what Joe wanted to do, and once he was in it, he realized he needed to stay with it because wrestling was over for him. But I'm pretty sure he continued to make a success out of it. It's a bit of a "dream vs. reality" situation, but it was a smart investment for him that required a whole lot of work.

Dick Murdoch had a bar called "Dick's Dive." If you think about it, what else are you going to call it? The "Gay Paree?" I'm not sure if it was a success, but, knowing Murdoch, it was a place where the boys sat and drank for free.

When Dick the Bruiser took to calling me Bobby when I first started, it was after a great manager named Bobby Davis. That was a treat for me, and I finally got to meet him when we were doing a WWF pay-per-view in California about 15 years ago. He lives in San Bernardino, and Vince McMahon had him sit in and call a match with Gorilla Monsoon and me. He made the most of his money and now owns 20 Wendy's restaurants around the country. But I don't think any of them serve wine.

Dick Garza, who was The Mighty Igor, used to live the gimmick of the stereotypical dumb Polish person. We used to say that he was the original Polish joke. He used to walk to the ring with nurses' shoes with long underwear and wrestling trunks over them. He wore this little hat and waved to the fans, smiling like he was mentally challenged.

He was as strong as a moose and a genius, too, when it came to the stock market. He never spent a dime on anything throughout his career. But he loved that gimmick of being dumb, and you would have never known how smart he was with money.

Other wrestlers had their share of investment success and failures. Baron Leoni owned a bunch of pizza restaurants. Jerry and Jack Brisco currently own a body shop in Tampa, Florida. Mike Gallagher owned a Shakey's pizza. The Bushwhackers had a restaurant in Tampa called— you guessed it—The Bushwhackers. It wasn't that successful, but they had a hell of a menu. They're wonderful guys and I really hoped it would do well for them.

A lot of wrestlers didn't realize that they should get into other businesses or invest. Maybe they didn't know how to. Many baseball players in the '30s and '40s went into farming after their careers were over, primarily because they were farmers before they were ballplayers, so they already knew that business.

I got into a seafood restaurant business when I was a minimal stock partner in a restaurant chain called Crabby Bills in St. Petersburg, Florida. The guy who ran the restaurant asked me, Brutus Beefcake, and the Bushwhackers to invest in it. It was great. They had a sign on the wall that said, "If you like home cooking, go home." Something that "The Brain" would say. It was successful, and I made money from that. I wasn't in control of the place and didn't have a say in anything, but I did go there and drink for nothing and sign a few autographs. It was fun, but I was luckier than others. To have a Bobby Heenan's Place, I'd have to supervise someone at the register and other things. It's too much work, and I'm just plain lazy. I don't want to work that hard.

I'm still batting around an idea for an Amish strip bar. It's called "Juggies and Buggies."

The smartest guy I know in this business who simply saved his money is Rene Goulet. He never worked on top, but he was a good hand and a good worker. The reason a guy doesn't work on top has nothing to do with ability, it's just that he is not at the right place at the right time. Sometimes, a promoter is not looking for what you are giving. Rene worked for all those years and saved his money and now he and his wife live well and have the best of everything. He didn't waste money in bars or on four new suits a week. He simply put his money away and is retired, living in a beautiful home, and playing golf every day.

That's the lesson. Just save your money. That's what it all comes down to. If you're not good at investing and don't trust others with your money, then leave it alone. Spend what you need to spend it on, but realize that saving is the best way to live the good life later. It's really as simple as that. The idea is to live the high life after you spend your life drinking the Miller High Life.

Or even Pabst Blue Ribbon and pot roast. When I traveled on the road, there would be guys in a car, and we all had just a little bit of money, again making that five-dollar bill every night. To save money on meals, we'd wrap a pot roast in tinfoil and put in some carrots and potatoes. We'd put it on the manifold of the car, drive about two hundred miles, pull over, and it would be cooked.

All the fans thought we hung out in fancy restaurants, smoking cigars, eating steaks, and drinking expensive champagne. That's a myth. It's usually a lot of Pabst and baloney. We'd call it the "Baloney Blowout." Other guys would order hot water in a diner because it was free. They would have a teabag with them or put ketchup in it to make tomato soup. They'd ask the waiter how much the bread or gravy cost.

Technically, it was free, so they'd order bread and gravy. I rarely ate late at night, because if I was driving, I'd just wanted to get home. Plus, eating a big meal at night made me sleepy.

A lot of the guys just didn't want to spend the money on food and that was smart. They would get some food and soda out of the machine—it was tough back then to watch what we ate. Today it's a lot easier, but not if you stop at a truck stop, where the food is reasonable too. They say truck drivers go to the place they know has the best food. Not true. They do it because it's cheap and they can get a lot of food. Think about it. Ever hear of a truck driver writing a cookbook?

I know others ate steak and lobster, including Gorilla Monsoon. Money was of no object to him, and he was a very generous man, but he made a lot of money. Most guys just went back to the hotel room and ordered pizza.

There were times when I would go to a nice restaurant. Gene Okerlund, Paul Orndorff, and I ate at The Palms. My wife and I ate at the top of the NBC Rainbow Room and the Tavern on the Green just to say we did it. But we didn't do it every night.

Years ago, I went to a fancy restaurant with Nick Bockwinkel, Ray Stevens, and Roger Kirby. Nick asked to see the wine steward, sounding like a big shot. "May I see your list?" he asked. I know Nick didn't know about wine, but he wouldn't admit it. No one did at our table, including me. If it doesn't have 20:20 at the end of the name, I have no idea if it's good or not. Maybe the wine steward was working us too and didn't know anything about wine. But he still suggested this fancy white wine made in 1941. Nick ordered it and I told the waiter to bring us all glasses and he poured. I was sitting next to Nick who was talking to Roger. When he wasn't looking, I switched my water glass for his wine glass. He took a drink and swished it from side to side like a wine-tasting connoisseur. He turned to me and said, "Rather mild."

I couldn't take it. "You asshole!" I yelled. "You're drinking water." He wouldn't sell the gag.

Look at all the people who win the lottery and have nothing when it's over. It all comes down to what you save. How do people go broke again after they have all that money? It's a sad and common fact of life. If you win $20 million and donate half to charity, pay your taxes, and help your friends out, you should have enough to live on for the rest of your life. How can people be broke after that?

I've dedicated a good amount of time to help out the wrestlers who have fallen on hard times. Sometimes, it was their fault and other times it was through no fault of their own. I'm on the board at Cauliflower Alley, and Mike Tenay and I emcee the annual banquet ever year. We pay our own way in, including airfare and hotel. No one there makes a dime, and all the money goes directly to those who need it.

I'll never forget what Wally Karbo once told me. It's a lesson that we can all learn from. He said, "Never loan anybody anything that you wouldn't give them. Because if they don't pay you back, so what? Be thankful that you can loan."

I hate loaning people money, because I hate to ask for it. I don't like to discuss business like that. I just like to laugh.

Maybe I should have been a circus clown with a red nose, a squirt bottle, and 15 guys with me in a Volkswagen.

CHAPTER 10

The Importance of Family

My mother, Millie, never beat me or yelled at me growing up. She did hit me once, but I was asking for it. When I was a kid, I was always told to be home by nine. Some of the other kids could stay out until 10, so I decided to follow the crowd.

I thought to myself, "What's going to happen? She may beat me. She'll eventually get tired of beating me, but I won't get tired of staying out late." When I got home an hour after I was supposed to, she was mad. She had this big ring on her finger and she hit me as I was putting my head down. She hit the top of my head, broke her finger, and never messed with me again.

Family should be very important to everyone. That's your safety net and where you should feel the most love and security. Some people come from very dysfunctional families, families with single parents, and even some families that are ashamed of certain members.

No matter what your family situation is, don't let your business life overtake your personal life, because if you do, you simply have no life. You only get one trip through this world, and then you die. Make it as easy as you can on yourself by getting along with your family. Eventually there will be a bunch of new people to take over, and that job you held or the money you made won't mean anything. How you treated your family will carry on forever.

"These things just come to me. Sometimes I feel like I have two brilliant minds."

I have three families that don't include the fictional "Bobby Heenan Family." I have my family, the set of friends who I grew up with who I consider my family, and my fraternity in wrestling. Those people are very important to me. Relationships mean everything.

When I grew up and well before that time, many felt that children should be seen and not heard. Women were not even treated with proper respect. My grandmother was German, as were her father and mother. She was born in 1883. Her dad would not allow his wife to eat at the table. She had to serve him and wait until he was done before she could eat. I can't imagine what kind of family life that would be. It's a terrible example to set for children, both male and female. You're teaching the son to treat his wife as a servant and the daughter to be a servant.

I think as the '40s and World War II came along, families drew a little closer together. In the '50s, there was the "Beaver Cleaver" mentality. I don't mean that in a negative way, even though I hated that show and that little bastard Beaver. In many ways, I wish society was still that way. It was great to see a guy come home to have dinner with a suit on and mom wearing the pearls while vacuuming or re-tarring the roof.

In the '60s, family life changed because of Vietnam and the assassination of President Kennedy. You know, I can't figure out what the big deal was about Kennedy. People just loved him, but he wasn't in office all that long and for pretty much his entire term, we were in a war in Vietnam. He and his brother were linked to Marilyn Monroe and other women. That means JFK wasn't faithful to his wife. It's been written that he was on all kinds of drugs for pain. Apparently, his father ripped off everybody when he sold whiskey. What do we really know about the guy that's good? All I've ever heard about is the bad and, frankly, I have little respect for him.

Respect is hard to come by, because one has to be willing to work hard for it. After the Vietnam War, I think people lost respect for authority because of Richard Nixon and how he had to resign because of the Watergate break in. Music, movies, magazines, and television were changing. Things were being stepped up a notch. Life changed. You no longer had to watch yourself to not say, "Damn it." It was getting to the point where you could say that and more. It has made our world a completely different place where respect is difficult to give and receive. Look at people walking down the street. Look at how people drive down the street. It is a different world.

I witnessed those changes when kids my age were starting to go off to war. I was supporting my mother and grandmother and kept getting deferments from the government because I was the sole supporter of my family. After a while, when they needed more troops, they changed the policy and said no more deferments. I had my friends write letters to a senator to keep me out because my mother and grandmother couldn't get along without me. It wasn't just a money issue. Neither of them could drive and they couldn't get around without me. They were elderly. Plus, our neighborhood was changing—and not for the better—and I was concerned. I couldn't go to Vietnam and leave them. They designated me 1Y. I wanted to be 16F, which I think is a hostage who is captured after the women and children.

I reapplied with an attorney and I got classified as 1F, which is a hardship case. But if I were forced to go, I would have had to. I wasn't going to go to Canada, shovel snow, and drink beer with a girl saying "eh" to me all night. There's something about a girl who wears sweatsocks in August that turns me off. I wasn't going to go to jail because that's harder to get out of. It's not that I was dedicated nor was I resigned to life in the military. In the army, I could always take a bump and fall off a tank and hurt my back. But I was very glad I got out of that service.

When I did go in for my army physical in 1966, I was already in the wrestling business. My hair was bleached blonde. Not many men had done that to their hair during that time. Jockey at that time made red bikini underwear that were just really small briefs. There I was, standing in front of this tough guy in a crew cut with bleached blonde hair and panties, trying desperately to talk in a low voice.

A buddy of mine even suggested that I get my blood pressure real high. But to do that, I would have needed to eat salt sandwiches. Have you ever tried to eat a goddamn salt sandwich? I ate half of one and got real sick and threw up. I don't think it can be done.

Not wanting to serve was not in any way an issue of patriotism. I love my country and would gladly serve it, but I had an obligation to my mother and grandmother. Besides, I don't like to see a guy hurt. I know that sounds strange coming from me, but that's true. I went to a lot of trouble to stay out. My main concern was not to hurt my mother. She had been through enough with my aunt dying of cancer and having to raise me without a father. I played a few pranks that got me in trouble, but never was in jail. I didn't go to school when I was enrolled in school, so I wasn't a model student. But I did work hard to support her.

I had respect for her because she would talk to me and tell me why she was upset with me. I really was concerned about her feelings and those of my grandmother. That probably kept me out of Leavenworth and San Quentin. People always wonder what makes a good parent. A good parent only needs a few qualifications. First, as a mother or father, you have to be able to talk *to* your child, not talk *at* them. If they banged up the car, do you think they meant to do it? No. Find out what happened. If they were negligent, then punish them. Parents nowadays are too worried about making their kids mad. Let them get mad. They'll get tired of it and get over it.

I chose to stay in Indianapolis after I started working for the AWA, which was based out of Minneapolis. In all the years I was with them, I had to pay my own transportation because I chose not to relocate. In the end, it was cheaper than moving my mother and grandmother there. I tried moving them to Minneapolis in 1969, but it only lasted a month after my grandmother fell down and broke her wrist, so I decided to take them back. They lived in an apartment, and it was too confining. They didn't know anybody or where anything was. Plus, they didn't drive.

I told Verne that I couldn't leave them, and I would just travel back and forth. He never offered me any help, and I didn't ask for it nor did I expect it. It was my own choice. If my payoff was $100 for a night's work, after expenses, I would be in the hole $50.

It was about sacrifice for me, and I was happy to do that. That's what family is for. I wouldn't let a promoter get to me, because my mother and grandmother were happy at home in Indianapolis and I wasn't dealing with snow up to my eyeballs in Minnesota. I gladly paid those expenses, whether I made any money or not.

During that time, I would just drive. Sometimes it was close by in Chicago or Moline, but when we had to go from Milwaukee to Denver, I couldn't drive. After flying to Denver, I'd have to fly to Minneapolis and do TV, fly to Milwaukee, catch a ride to Chicago, and then fly to Indy. No one else lived in Indianapolis, so I was usually on my own there. It got pretty expensive.

On April 9, 1979, my mother Millie passed away. When I heard about it, I wanted to remember her as the last time I saw her alive. I'm like that with everyone, and that's why I don't look at dead bodies. At the time she died, I was working with the NWA and commuting from Indianapolis to Atlanta and back. My wife called me at 3:00 in the morning and told me that she had to take my mother to the hospital.

She had heart failure before and was admitted to the hospital prior to that last time. On that day, I was told that they served her chili for lunch in spite of her illness. She was a heart patient eating chili, because that's what she wanted. She also made it crystal clear that she wanted her own room. She had to share her television with another woman in the room, but she kept control of the remote, changing the channels whenever she wanted and keeping the volume very high. My mom and her roommate were fighting all day, so I got my mother a private room, which is what she wanted all along. She was happy and everything was nice and quiet for her.

I had to get a flight from Atlanta to Minneapolis. My wife picked me up at the airport and we immediately went to the hospital, because my mother was in intensive care at that point. When we arrived, a woman came out and took me into a special room and told me that the doctor was coming in to talk to me. It never crossed my mind that she had died. I thought they were coming in to ask for my permission to operate. A woman came in and I didn't even pay attention that she had a cross on her pocket. She told me that they brought my mother in and they were able to stabilize her, but then she quickly deteriorated and expired.

They gave me my mom's belongings to take home. It was a Seiko watch, a nightgown, and her housecoat. That's when her death really hit me. I was leaving the hospital with a paper bag of my mother's belongings. I thought to myself, "After a full life, this is all that was left behind after she left this world."

I went home and I told Jessica, who by then was four months old, "Grammy is gone, but she'll always be with us."

I made the arrangements, but Cindi had to go identify her because I couldn't look at her. She told me that she had just given Millie a permanent the night before, and I still wonder if the fumes had an effect on her condition. I never had a viewing for her. Again, I wanted to remember her how she was when she was alive, dressing weird and beaning me on the head with a ring. Friends of mine drove in from Florida and Indianapolis. I buried her the next day at a graveside service without any type of viewing.

I remembered what my mother once told me, "I don't want no funeral. I don't want flowers. I don't want anything. What good does it do you, Ray? Nothing. What good does it do to me? Nothing. But it makes the florist rich. It makes the funeral director rich. It makes Hallmark and everyone else rich.

"It's over."

She's been gone for a long time now, but she'll always be alive in me, just like I told Jess. I just buried her shell, that's it. Every time I'm in Indianapolis, I go to the cemetery and I talk to her and my grandmother, who is buried next to her. It doesn't bother me. I'm not grieving her.

I talk to my mother every day, and I know she's around. I just know it. If I trip, I say, "Goddamn it, Millie. Quit it." I know she's always up to something. If we hear a noise in the middle of the night, my wife will say, "That's Millie, isn't it?" I think that happens in everyone's home.

Things happen that you just can't explain. In our house, we blame it on my mom. And that's how I get through grief and tragedy. I make light of it and realize that there is nothing I can do about it. It's not that I'm insensitive. I just move on. I don't see the point of sitting in a funeral home for three days, crying and wailing over the loss. I prefer to celebrate the life. And what a life Millie had.

But that's me. Everyone has to make his own decisions. Some people feel you should pay respects and mourn, and I respect that. But when I think about it, you go into the funeral home and sit there and cry. Then you walk slowly to the hearse. Then you drive slowly to the cemetery. Then you walk slowly to the gravesite. Why go through all those extremely slow steps of grief?

I shed a few tears when my mother died and I still miss her to this day. But I know what kind of life she lived, and I was glad I was able to help. I did everything I could do to help her and show my love for her. There are people out there who lose someone close to them without helping them in life or simply telling them how much they love them. After this cancer, I've learned how fragile life is and that you have to tell people how you feel about them. It seems easy and obvious to say, but so many people don't bother. I loved and respected my mother and she knew it. That made my life while she was alive and complete. I hope it did the same for her. I hope she respected me as well.

There's that word again. Respect. I would hope that Millie would also approve of how I took care of my family after she died. I have tried to do right by them as I did with her. But I also had the benefit of witnessing many examples of families who have stayed together in good times and in bad and have been great examples on how to treat my own family.

The Poffos are a great example of true family. Angelo, his lovely wife Judy, and their sons, Randy (Savage) and Lanny, are all very family-oriented. The sons are concerned about their parents and the parents are always concerned about their sons' and their futures. They always have been and always will be.

Randy was a ball player and played in the minor leagues for the Cincinnati Reds and the Chicago White Sox before he got into the wrestling business. Lanny was a gymnast and a poet in addition to being a great wrestler, although he never achieved the success that Randy did. Angelo and Judy went to DePaul University in Chicago and were college sweethearts. They are some of the most educated people I know. But what I love about all of them is that the Poffos have very strong family values.

What keeps their family together is the love and respect they have for each other, and it works. I get to see that often as Angelo lives down the street from me. Every so often, we sit by the pool, have a beer, and talk.

The only reason Angelo stayed in wrestling and ran a promotion was to get work for his sons when no one else would book them. He sacrificed his whole life for those boys when he could have easily retired and gotten out of the business. He was running a promotion that covered Tennessee and Kentucky, and they all wrestled in towns where there were no maps to find them and no roads to get there. Angelo would referee the preliminary matches and wrestle in the main event under a mask against Randy. Randy would trade outfits later on and wear a mask to wrestle in other matches. One of the Poffos would take tickets. One would put up posters to advertise the match. Angelo hustled to keep those boys in the business and working. He never gave up on his kids.

Some parents would discourage their kids from getting into the business. But it made them better people for the experience. They developed such strong work ethics. They were always on time and never late. When they said they would pay, they paid on time and with the amount they promised. And, on the other side, they would all give 100 percent effort if a promoter held up to his end of a deal.

Another dedicated family in this business is obviously the McMahon family. I don't use the term lightly or loosely, but Vince McMahon is a genius who has allowed the business to consume him. I don't mean that in a negative way. I don't think that man has been to bed since 1958. When I would go to an arena, I thought I was getting there early, but when I got there, he was already there. He'd been there for hours. He's engulfed himself in his business. He loves the WWE. He loves creating. He loves the marketing aspect. He loves dealing with the talent. He loves the television end of things and all the production. And he loves to be on stage.

Most importantly, he loves his family and has involved them in the business with him. His wife, Linda, son, Shane, and daughter, Stephanie are all active in WWE and are very good at what they do. They spend a great deal of time together, which I think can be a very positive thing. And since they have all worked together for so long, they are doing something right in separating their personal lives from their professional lives.

In the end, what I learned from family is one simple thing. The only thing that I can control is the ability to love and protect my family. That's what you learn on the streets, and the significance of that is something no one can ever teach you, whether in school or on the streets. You have to protect yourself and those you love, whether you belong to the Poffo family, the McMahon family, or the Heenan family (no, not the one you're thinking of). That's how I've tried to live my life and I highly recommend it.

CHAPTER 11

Love and Marriage... and Communication

My wife and I got in an argument one day—well, not just one day. I told her—and this is a line you can use with your spouse—"Hey, if you could have done any better, you would have. This is as good as you can do. You had enough time. You said 'yes' when I asked you. I didn't say 'yes.' You didn't ask me. This is the best you can do."

"I didn't have time to shop," she said.

Believe me, both men and women do a lot of "shopping," but some of it goes on in the dollar store.

I really don't mean to continually knock on the wrestling business, but it can make you irritable. Any job can do that when the hours are long and you're traveling constantly. Professional wrestling takes you away from home. And, when you finally get home after days or weeks on the road, you don't want to be "romantic." The laundry needs to be done and bills need to be paid. There is a lot of stuff you have to do. You don't have time to take your wife out to dinner, but you should because she made dinner all week for the family. Show some consideration and take her out. Just because you ate in a restaurant for weeks doesn't mean that she doesn't deserve a night at one. Be considerate. Some people aren't that considerate, and they simply don't get it.

"I know all about cheating. I've had six very successful marriages."

If I don't know how my wife is feeling, it's because she doesn't tell me. I may be "The Brain," but I'm not a mind reader. For instance, if she doesn't like me wearing my shoes to bed every night, I'm not going to know that unless she tells me. That's what happens in relationships. People don't communicate. If my wife says, "Honey, take the wing tips off. You're ruining the sheets," I'll take them off. It makes sense.

Most people won't tell you how they feel and you never know. For some people, even if they are told, are they even listening? That's another thing people don't do in life. They don't listen. Like Judge Judy says, "You're not receiving." You have to receive. Otherwise how do you know what to talk about? If you're lying, how do you know how to defend yourself? If you're telling the truth, you want to hear them or "receive," so you can tell the truth. You just have to listen. Open your ears.

Communication—both talking and receiving—is so important. You have to have it in a family. You can't all sit around the macaroni and cheese and weinies and talk, especially if people are in three different rooms with four different television sets. One's in dance. One's in soccer. One's in drug detox. You have to sit down and really talk to each other. And you have to listen.

The most valuable thing that I have gained over the past few years is patience (which I have now and never had before), the ability to communicate, and the ability to listen. Instead of fighting and arguing, I just want to work things out.

Just because you have the ability to both talk and listen, doesn't mean you should do more of one than the other. When you talk, you're not listening. And, if you don't listen, you're not hearing what that person said. If you sit there like a lug and just nod your head like a dope without saying a word, you're not helping to communicate.

But with communication comes honesty. Yet honesty can truly strain a relationship just as much, if not more so than lying. Sometimes people don't want to tell the truth about something. That's the third component that goes with communicating and listening—just sit down and talk and be honest—not to mention shutting up and listening. Don't get mad about honesty until you know everything. In the end, it doesn't help anything. It just raises your blood pressure and makes you drink more.

If you talk, listen, and maintain honesty, you can gain a better understanding of the person you're with. Many men feel that motherhood is an easy job, where a woman just sits at home watching the soaps and eating bonbons. That's not how it is. It is not like going to a job eight hours a day and then going back at her job. A mother is always home. A mother doesn't go out to lunch and hang out at the water cooler so she can stare at Myrna's ass and tell dirty stories. A stay-at-home mom has the same job for years and the job is always with her.

A mother who stays at home has a lot more to do. Her job is different every day. She has kids to take care of and kids who need to get to school. If one has a sore throat, she has to take him to the doctor. She has to cook the meals. Then, when her husband gets home, he complains how tired he is. But he only did one thing. What a bite in the ass. A woman—or in this day and age, whichever parent is staying home—has to give a lot more because they have to do a lot more. Whoever is at home has to make the spouse understand that by communicating honestly and with open ears, so they can understand that. Explain it clearly, don't yell, and don't throw the lukewarm TV dinner on the plate.

While there were different experiences in professional wrestling, there were many times when it was the same routine over and over again just like any job. When I was in Georgia in 1979 from February to December, I had one day off every week. I also went to the same towns every week. Monday was Augusta, Tuesday was Macon, Wednesday was Columbus, Thursday was Rome or Athens, Friday was Atlanta, Saturday we had TV in the morning and a spot show in Carrollton, and Sunday was in Marietta. On Monday, you'd start all over again.

Every work day, I'd leave at three in the afternoon, and I'd usually get home by about one in the morning. I'd sleep until 9 or 10 and I'd have the whole day with my wife and daughter until about 3 or 4. So, you see, I had a family life, but I also had another life where I rode with a bunch of guys in a car. Just like family, we protected each other, whether it was an irate fan attacking someone or wrestling someone and just not wanting to hurt him. Hell, you didn't want to get hurt either, but you protected each other in and outside that ring, just as you would protect your family and your loved ones at home.

But there were rarely any discussions about our family at home when we rode in cars and talked about things. We focused our conversation mainly on business and rarely on family. Mostly, we'd get in the car and bitch about the promoter. He had a big house on the lake, and we didn't. We probably weren't the only ones bitching. I'm sure back home, someone was bitching about her husband being gone, or something to do with the butcher, the milkman, the neighbor, or the PTA meeting.

Much like any other job, it is like you live two different lives. I'm relieved to get home from hearing bitching about the promoter, riding in a car, showering with a bunch of naked men, wearing spandex, and bleaching my hair. I have to walk through that door, pretend that I'm Beaver's dad, and be nice to my family. If my wife asked me how things went, how my match was, and what we talked about in the car, I certainly don't want to bring that home to her. A lot of guys get divorced because they bring their jobs home. They didn't get the raise they were promised. So-and-so got the big sale, and they didn't. Work problems are work problems. Home problems are home problems. Don't mix up the two.

But I'll also tell you that something I don't want to hear at 2 a.m. after getting hit in the head with the chair and putting down a 12-pack is my wife telling me, "The butcher screwed the chops up."

"Well, there's not much I can do about it at 2 a.m. Go shake and bake the cat. Leave me alone."

There's a time and place for everything. Couples need to be respectful of that. If you're out of the house all the time, be attentive when you get home. If you're attending to the house, then be understanding and try to resolve problems. Couples need each other, but they also need their independence.

It was rough for many guys trying to get used to the life of a professional wrestler. Luckily, I was on the road before I was married and had a kid, otherwise I don't know how I would have adjusted to going on the road after being married for years and staying at home in a different job. I didn't know the difference. I didn't get married until I was 34, and I already had many years in the business. I don't know how I would have felt getting married before getting into the business and then having to go on the road and be away. I guarantee you that I probably would not have liked it and may not have done it for very long.

It was very hard not being around my daughter, but the most I was ever gone was a month and that was in Japan. It took two months to get over the trip and during the trip, I missed my family. When my daughter was a baby, I wanted to be home more, but I couldn't be. But I prepared myself for it. I told myself that when I had a kid, I would probably be away from her for certain periods of time. It comes with the territory. And I wasn't going to treat her like she was an anchor or an inconvenience that hurt my career.

People complain about having kids, because it affects their personal and business life. No shit. When that child comes into this world, he or she is innocent and deserves your full attention, whether you're tucking the kid in or calling at night from the road. If you have a kid and then decide you don't like it very much, maybe you should have taken a pill. It's called an aspirin and you hold it between your knees.

The travel in wrestling killed a lot of marriages. What usually happened was the guy would come home after being on the road and then listen to a wife who would do nothing but bitch about him being gone. Nothing is said about being glad to see each other again after a long time.

The problems only get worse if a wrestler's payoffs are low and he isn't bringing home a whole a lot of money. I believe that once things get to that point, there must have been problems existing before that. As the marriage unravels, divorce seems inevitable. They don't communicate or talk and they drift apart. He calls her a bitch and she calls him an asshole.

Many people I knew both in and out of the wrestling business gave up on their marriages. They would end up in divorce court and say, "I was married to him for 20 years, and I knew from the first day I met him that he was no good."

Now, if I were the judge, I'd say, "Then why would you spend 20 years with him, sitting and sleeping on rented furniture? Was the sex that good? For 20 years of misery, are you nuts?"

From the first day my wife Cindi met me, she may not have known what she was in store for, and sometimes I would be up to no good, playing pranks and embarrassing her. But I wouldn't have changed that day for anything.

I met my wife, Cindi, in 1974. I came up to Minnesota to work for the AWA. Many of the wrestlers and I would hang out at this bar called the Left Guard owned by Fuzzy Thurston and Max McGhee. I got to know the guys, and they had a real nice place. It had a disco and separate rooms for Italian food, Chinese food, and steak. Fuzzy and Max knew all the wrestlers, and they would never charge us a cover. So, obviously it became a favorite hang-out for the boys. The nice thing was that there was always a bunch of women there. Talk about a meat house.

One day in October, I was there with Billy Graham and Ray Stevens and we were having a drink after the matches. This friend of mine, Tom, and his wife, Karen, were there with another guy and this woman, who turned out to be Cindi. My friends came over and introduced me to Cindi and her date.

We all sat together, talked, and had a few drinks. They invited me to Mamalu's, which was a rib joint, to have dinner. We went over there and I sat directly across from Cindi. I had a few scotches as the evening wore on, and we were telling stories and having a lot of laughs. I liked Cindi. She was a very pretty Italian woman. I liked the way she talked. The timing was perfect as she wasn't married at the time, and I was just coming off a breakup. It wasn't really important who I broke up with. She saved me from buying a Christmas gift.

I started talking with Cindi. Her date was a bodybuilder, and he was complaining about an upset stomach or something like that. Big baby. During that time, the hotels would host Sunday afternoon parties when the Minnesota Vikings were playing. I was invited to a party hosted by

Chuck Foreman and Stu Voigt, who played for the Vikings. I asked Cindi if she wanted to come with me. She said, "Yes, I'll meet you at the Left Guard."

She wouldn't give me her address and phone number, so I didn't know if she would show or not. Not that giving me her address would have helped. I can get lost in a phone booth with good directions. She showed up and we went to the party at the hotel, watched the game, and had some drinks. Later, we spent some time at the Left Guard and had a few more drinks.

I was staying in a hotel at the time. I asked her, "Would you like to come upstairs to my room and watch a little TV?"

"No," she said.

"Would you like to go out again?"

"Yes," she said and gave me her address and phone number. We kissed goodbye.

The next time I was in town, I called her and invited her out to dinner. We went out with the couple, Tom and Karen, who introduced us. We went to a nice restaurant and a couple of nice bars. We started developing a pattern in our dates. Every time, the night would end with me asking, "Would you like to watch a little TV in my room?" And she would always say, "No," and then go home.

This went on for six months. I couldn't get her in my room if I offered her a hundred bucks and told her I was a Shriner. I started to think about doing things the old-fashioned way, and take a doorknob, put it in a wool sock, and knock her out. I thought to myself, "I've gone through too much prime rib and booze with her. She's coming upstairs or I'm going."

In spite of the way we ended our dates, we were getting along great. Once again, we stood in the lobby of my hotel and I asked her, "Do you want to go up to my room and watch TV?"

She said, "Yes."

I thought I was getting worked by her. I took her upstairs and she went into the bathroom. True to my word, I started watching TV. She came out of the bathroom and sat on the edge of the bed. True to my word, I watched TV. We watched TV and after awhile, she went home. While we took things to another level after a while, I still got her that night. Like I said, I was true to my word. I asked her if she wanted to watch TV, and that's exactly what we did on that first night.

I asked her on one of our dates, "What made you like me?"

"I never met anyone that could talk like you and make people laugh," she said. "You ought to write a book."

And here I am, writing this book for my fans and you deadbeats who mooch it off my fans. I have no idea why she is still with me.

I do things to her just to drive her nuts. On our refrigerator, we have a list of things we will need from the store. It would say, "Bread, milk, eggs," that kind of thing. But I'd add things like "Weiner Helper."

And, remember guys, the more you know, the more your wife will make you do. If you screw everything up, she'll never make you do it again.

Chances are that when you date someone, you're not going to get married. Enjoy each other's company. Don't put the burden of "maybe getting married" on anybody too soon. Don't feel that you have to see each other every day. You can smother them really easily. People need room to breathe.

Do your own thing. Be independent, even when you're married. Communicate and talk things out. Violence is not the answer, unless you're living next to Beaver Cleaver. God, I wanted to choke that little bastard.

If you do find someone special and get married, for God's sake, don't cheat on them. You may pass up a lot of beautiful women and handsome men and a lot of great opportunities. But, if you're human, you'll feel guilty about it. When I was younger and on the road, there were a lot of women out there. It was like a garage sale. It was like being a Chicago Cub and hitting a ball at Wrigley Field. Hit it high and watch it fly. Get as much action as you can, is the motto I lived by. But with my luck, some son of a bitch in the stands would catch that ball and prevent me from winning that World Series, if you know what I mean.

Once you get married, care about your spouse all the time—not just when you feel like it—and realize where you are in life and what your true responsibility is. You have a responsibility to your family and friends not to be a lowlife and a womanizer. God knows I've seen my share of them. Trust me, that's no way to live your life. Some strange woman won't make you a man. The measure of a man comes from acting like a human being.

If you have a thought in your mind of, "Maybe I shouldn't do this" or "I really don't want to do this," then don't. If you think, "I should have done that, but..." then you shouldn't have done it. Always be sure of what you're going to do. These women who wait for the boys in the hotel rooms may never be seen or heard from again, so why start anything? Or worse, they may get pregnant, and then not only do you get obligated financially, but you're obligated to support and see that kid. And if you don't, the kid misses out and you miss out, all because of one stupid mistake.

In marriage, understand from the beginning, guys, that you don't mean anything if your wife does everything around the house. All you do is bring in the big check. They make sure the kids get fed in the morning and off to school. You can get a job any place, but you can only get a family in one place. Remember that nice life you have, your wife has it too. In my business, all the guys thought about sometimes were the towns they had to make when there were many more important things in life. Whether your job is wrestling, accounting, or oiling up those nudie girls, your family is more important.

When my daughter was getting married, I was nervous about what I had to do and where I had to go. She gave me some great advice. "FM"—Follow Mommy.

That's the truth. If your wife runs the household, let her do it her way. She doesn't come to your job and show you how to make the slurpees at the 7-Eleven. They say home is where the heart is, but it's more than that. Home is where everything is, or should be. I don't want to sound sexist, but women handle those types of major responsibilities better than men. It's not that I think they should do everything around the house, but I was raised by my mother and grandmother and saw the great job they did. I didn't have a father who pitched in or was even around. Besides, the reason God created women to have babies is that God knew they could handle it. Men couldn't. We can barely shave our necks and if we nick ourselves, we consider that pain. I know that the job housewives do is something I could never do. Not because of gender, but because of ability.

Cindi and I dated about five years before I proposed. At the time, she was a buyer for K-Tel Records and she was transferred to Indianapolis where I lived. She had an apartment right down the street from me. I was still working in Minnesota and all over the AWA territory, so I'd see her a couple of days a week, and she would visit my mother.

I called her from Denver to propose to her. "I'll answer when we get to your home. I want to do this face to face with your mother right there," she said. "I don't believe you. You're ribbing me."

Now why would she think that?

I got off the plane and she still wasn't convinced. She said, "I told you that I won't answer you until you get home in front of your mother."

We arrived at my house and I announced to my mother that I was asking Cindi to marry me. My mother sat on the couch without saying a word. I had another surprise for her. I said, "You're going to be a grandmother too, Millie."

I had been working in Hawaii for about a year with Lord James Blears. I took Cindi with me on one trip, and that's where she got pregnant with Jessica. She told me, "Jessica went to Hawaii coach and came back first class."

My mom was quiet for a while.

"Is she gonna live here?"

"Yes," I said.

She lit up a cigarette and watched TV without saying a word.

"What's wrong?" I asked her.

"Usually when a son gets married, they leave," she said. "I thought I could unload your dead ass."

Good old Millie. That was her idea of giving us her blessing.

We got married in Indianapolis at a condo I had. The night we got married, we went to this place that I rented where we had a bar, food, music, and everything. Afterwards, Cindi and I were ready for our honeymoon. The two of us, along with a buddy of mine named Buster, went to the Twin Drive-In on the south side of Indianapolis right next to a factory.

We bought a case of beer, a sack of beer nuts, and Slim Jims and we went to the show. Boy, I know how to live it up and show a girl—not to mention my new wife—a good time. Cindi sat in back, and Buster and I sat up front with the top down on my convertible. We saw *Meat Cleaver Massacre* and *Amuck*. One of them was about a bunch of midgets who raped a cheerleader on a grease rack of a gas station. Real romantic stuff.

We all eventually fell asleep. When we woke up to leave at about 3 a.m., there was soot all over all of us from the factory next door.

That was my honeymoon. Watching *Meat Cleaver Massacre* and *Amuck* with Buster. I've told other people that my honeymoon was a "Loser Leaves Town" cage match and I got to stick around.

It may not have been fancy. It sure as hell wasn't Hawaii. But we were together and we had fun. More couples should feel that way. As long as you're with your spouse, where you are isn't as important. Okay, maybe I should have had better taste in my selection of movies, but I know Buster enjoyed it.

Before Cindi moved in, my mother and I ate pretty simple foods such as meat loaf, baloney, eggs, and Pepsi. Quite a diet. When Cindi did move in after the wedding, she started buying all these different foods that we weren't used to, like chicken breasts and fish. Boy, she could really cook.

I got home one day and my mother said, "I don't like her. I want you to kick her out."

"Mom, I'm married to Cindi now."

"Yeah, but she changed my whole kitchen around. She's moving everything around."

I played along, "You know what, Mom, you're right. I'll grab her by the ass of her pants and throw her out on the lawn. Then I'll pack up her bags and throw them out too. She can just call herself a cab and get home the best way she can."

"Yeah, do it," my mom said.

"I'll pick her up, throw her on the lawn, and tell her it's over," I said.

"That's right, you and me."

"No trouble, Millie."

I start to walk out and she stopped me, "Wait a minute, let's see what she's making for dinner tonight."

Everything was fine after that. I just went along with her. It was pointless to argue, and it wouldn't have done any good. My mom learned to share me with another woman.

CHAPTER 12

Kids and What They Teach Us

Y*ou wonder sometimes what parents say to their kids behind closed doors, especially about me. That's why when a kid would approach me for an autograph and I knew it was actually for his mom or dad, I would write, "Tell your parents to teach you better manners" without signing it.*

I was doing an autograph signing and this little kid came up, leaning at the table. He was staring at me for the longest time. I would sign autographs and look up. There he was, still staring at me.

Finally, his parents walked up. He turned to them and said, "He's not a prick."

There's three things you should never do in life: go in the kitchen of your favorite Chinese restaurant, see what your daughter is wearing when she leaves the house, or see what she does after she leaves the house. That's too much aggravation for any one person.

When my wife was pregnant, we were asked to take these Lamaze courses. Since I had to work all the time, I never made the classes. When it came time to deliver, I brought a survival kit with me so I could get through the day. It was a suitcase with a bottle of Scotch, a roll of dimes, a phone book, and Fig Newtons. The Newtons were for Cindi because

"Money's the same, whether you earn it or scam it."

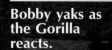

Bobby yaks as the Gorilla reacts.

Left to right are Bobby, Nick Bockwinkel, and Ray Stevens.

Bobby at one of his many Fan Fest appearances.

November 8, 2003

B∗T∗W

Fremont Mariott

btwrestling.com

BIG TIME WRESTLING'S

FAN FEST 2003

Bob Orton   Bret "Hitman" Hart   Jim "The Anvil" Neidhart   Nick Bockwinkel   Bobby "The Brain" Heenan
The Hart Foundation

CHAIR SHOTS
AND OTHER OBSTACLES

Bobby with Pepper Gomez and Nick Bockwinkel.

"The Brain" looks after his charge.

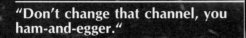

"Don't change that channel, you ham-and-egger."

Bobby with Miguel Alonzo.

Getting ready for an interview.

CHAIR SHOTS
AND OTHER OBSTACLES

Bobby awaiting his next victim.

Bobby greeting John Tolos.

Bobby with Mike Tenay co-hosting Cauliflower Alley.

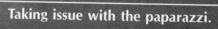

Taking issue with the paparazzi.

CHAIR SHOTS AND OTHER OBSTACLES

F.O.B. - Friends of Bobby (l. to r. Don Leo Jonathan, The Destroyer, Nick Bockwinkel, and Jack Brisco).

Dr. Mike Lano (wrealano@aol.com)

Dr. Mike Lano (wrealano@aol.com)

"The Brain" basking in the boos.

A mischievous Bobby checking if there is any life on "the moon."

"What are you looking at, humanoid?"

Bobby with Roger Kent, the voice of the AWA.

CHAIR SHOTS
AND OTHER OBSTACLES

Bobby and his crown jewel, AWA World Champ Nick Bockwinkel.

Bobby being inducted into the Cauliflower Ring of Friendship (l. to r. Red Bastein, Bobby, Ray Stevens, and Karl Lauer of Cauliflower Alley).

Dr. Mike Lano (wrealano@aol.com)

Dr. Mike Lano (wrealano@aol.com)

Background photo by Tedd Webb

she loved them. The dimes and the phone book were to make calls to people after the birth. The Scotch was there to steady my dialing hand.

The doctor asked me to put "the greens" on. When I finally figured out what the hell he was talking about, I put them on. Then I told him that I had never been to the Lamaze meetings. He said, "You don't have to do anything, but it could be gory. Would it bother you?"

"I've seen Andre the Giant and Sky Low Low naked," I informed him.

He said, "What?"

"Never mind."

All the doctor told me to do was stand behind the bed and be there for moral support, so that's what I did. In between doing her breathing exercises, Cindi would sit back.

"Do you want a Newton?" I asked.

"I don't want a Newton."

She'd breathe some more and then sit back.

"Do you want a Newton?"

"No, I don't want a Newton."

It wasn't too bad, considering I didn't know what I was doing and was forcing cookies on my wife. Finally it was time to deliver and out came Jessica. Naturally, anyone would look to see what the baby was—a boy or a girl. We had been talking "boy" the whole time and even called "him" Jasper. I looked at the baby and she was swollen in her private area. Honestly, I thought she had testicles.

I was in a panic and said to Cindi, "There's no prick. There's no prick."

She said, "What?"

I said, "No prick."

She said, "No prick?"

The doctor said, "What?"

I said, "No prick."

He said, "Get back behind the bed. It's a girl."

So I stood back behind the bed and kept my mouth shut. I had a girl. A healthy girl. When I called people, I couldn't even tell them I had a girl. I would get as far as, "We had a baby," and I'd start crying. I was so happy. It was such an incredible moment, an event that I allowed to change my life. Some parents have babies and go back to the way they were, not letting that new life change their existing lives. That's not the way it works. Everything in your life changes from that moment on. Your routine and your priorities change. If they don't and you don't allow it to, you shouldn't have bothered to have a kid in the first place.

Remember the aspirin.

To tell you the truth, I'm glad I didn't have a boy. Some guys would want their name to continue, but I had to be practical about a Raymond Heenan Jr. or even a Bobby Heenan Jr. With my genes and me not being home, he would hopefully be eligible for parole about now. Or he would have been the first kid to get the electric chair at four years of age. They would have probably hung him in a gas chamber over the electric chair and then given him the lethal injection. Just to make sure.

We left the hospital in December, around the first day of winter. I had purchased a 1967 Ford Mustang convertible with a white top and blue body. I knew the guard out front and asked if I could keep the car running because it was cold.

They brought Cindi and Jess down in a wheelchair. Jess was wearing what I call her traveling suit, a red and white striped suit and a matching hat with a ball. I picked her up and put her in the front seat of the car. The heater was going full blast just for her. I walked to the other side of the car, got in, and took off. About five blocks down the road, I realized that I had forgotten Cindi.

I drove back and there she was, sitting in her wheelchair with her coat collar up and her hair blowing in the wind.

"Forgot me, huh?" she said between shivering.

I said, "No, Jess wanted to go for a spin around the parking lot."

She didn't find me all that funny at that moment.

We were finally home, two days after having the baby. I took Jess and handed her to my mother. Cindi walked in, looking very sore from the whole experience. Instead of saying, "Congratulations, it's a girl. How do you feel?" Millie said, "What's for dinner? I haven't had anything for two days."

Cindi didn't find her all that funny at that moment either. For a while, we were back to meatloaf, baloney, eggs, and Pepsi.

I bought my wife a wooden rocking chair so she could rock the baby in it. What I didn't know is that it is hard for a new mother to sit real well right after giving birth. So I bought this inner tube thing for Cindi to sit on. But leave it to my mom. When Cindi would get up to go to the bathroom, Millie would let the air out of the inner tube. A Heenan through and through.

But she wasn't done there. One day, she said to me, "Here's a hundred bucks. Go buy Cindi that warm-up suit I saw at the store."

"Really?" I asked.

"Yes, she told me she liked it."

I went out and spent the hundred bucks on the suit. Cindi got home and I gave it to her, telling her it was from mom. She broke down and started crying. "What a nice thing to do," she said. She loved that suit.

The next day, she left town for work. When she got to where she was going, she noticed there was a hundred bucks missing from her purse.

When I confronted my mom about it, she said, "Anything that's left on my counter is mine."

After Jessica was born, I went shopping and bought everything she needed like a fur coat and diamond rings. My life and my shopping habits changed. I used to buy her designer dresses until Cindi told me, "No, go to Wal-mart." She was absolutely right. I soon realized that babies grow about a half-inch a week and they throw up and shit on their clothes anyway, no matter where it was purchased and how much it cost. In fact, I swear they prefer to puke and shit all over the expensive stuff.

As Jessica grew up, she learned more about what I did for a living. A major issue came up about my name. My real name is Raymond, but my gimmick name is Bobby, and that's the name she knew me by. I figured it was time to explain it to her. No more kayfabing her.

Just as an aside for those who don't know or who may be a deadbeat bumming this book off someone and never bought the first one, "kay-fabe" is an expression in the wrestling industry that basically means "shut up, there are others around." It is used in case there is a "mark" around and you don't want to smarten them up to the wrestling business.

You use it to get rid of somebody, because if you talk to some of them openly about the business, you'll never get rid of them. I hate to be rude to people, but I have done it. I have no idea where the term "kay-fabe" came from, but Gorilla Monsoon had it as his vanity plate on his car. When Nick Bockwinkel and I bought a condo together, we called it "Kayfabe Kondo."

As I was driving my now eight-year-old daughter from school to dance, it was on my mind that I really should eventually tell her my real name, which I hadn't done up to that point. I was real nervous.

"Jessica," I said. "Have you ever heard people call me Ray?"

"Yes."

"Well, honey, that is my real name."

She paused for a minute.

"Does Mom know?" she asked.

"Yes, Mom knows," I reassured her. "But I changed my name at the beginning of my career so the 'Ray Heenan' part of me could live a normal life. My name was changed by someone else," referring to Dick The Bruiser.

I continued, almost in tears, "But our friends and the other kids, they don't need to know."

I was so scared as to how she was going to react. I was ready to cry. Had I deceived her all these years for not telling her my real name?

Would she look at me as a stranger? Would she ever trust me again? Would this forever change my relationship with my only child? I didn't know what to say, so I decided to be direct and honest.

"So, Jessica. My real name is Ray, not Bobby."

"And mom knows?" she asked again.

"Yes, Mom knows."

She thought about it for a few seconds, then my eight-year-old daughter—who I was worried that I had traumatized—said, "Okay, I'll kayfabe it, dad."

What the hell was I worried about? The kid was smarter than me. I guess I'm glad she didn't say, "Oh daddy, don't be a mark."

My wife constantly says, "I'm going to have myself tested for DNA, because I don't think Jessica is mine."

Jessica is me. Poor thing.

Jessica and I constantly play a game with people that drives them nuts. I'd be sitting on the couch with my daughter sitting next to me. Then I would ask her to leave the room and tell the other person to touch something in the room. Let's say they touched a table while she was out. She'd come back in and would be able to tell what was touched without seeing what happened.

I'd say, "Jessica, did he touch that bag?"

"No," she'd say confidently.

"Did he touch the lamp?"

"No."

"Did he touch the clock?"

"No."

"Did he touch the table?"

"Yes."

Our secret was we would mention a black object before the thing that was touched. The clock was black, so the next thing I said after that would be the object touched. We drove people nuts at parties.

I think the most important thing I have with my daughter is the sense of humor we share and the fun we have. She is identical to me. We like to go to the department stores together. She would be a lookout for me as I would take the hair off the female mannequin and put it on the male mannequin. She would unzip the pants of the male mannequin and pull the shirt out of the pants of the man through the zipper. We'd pose him like a woman. With the wig, the mannequin would look like Liz Taylor. After we were done doing our damage, we would just sit back on a bench and watch people react. She even pretended to be a store mannequin in a store window from time to time.

I taught my daughter to observe life just like I have. Stop and smell the roses or watch people trip over them. You don't need great wisdom to pass on to your child. A few pointers here and there, but mainly have fun with them. Parents spend so much time being authority figures that they don't spend time just having fun with their kids. It can be anything from throwing a ball around to messing with mannequins.

Whenever I was in a store, I would try to hide my identity with a ballcap or something, especially during the time that the WWF was hot. Inevitably, we would hear someone say, "Isn't that Bobby Heenan?"

That was our signal. Immediately, Jessica and I would start speaking gibberish, almost a different language. Then we'd hear, "No, it can't be. They're foreigners."

She is truly my buddy. I told her once, "You can have anything you want in life. I won't spoil you, but I will pamper you." You see, if something is spoiled, that means it's green and it stinks, kind of like a wrestler just starting out, a lot of guys I faced in the ring, or Dick the Bruiser's jock strap that he never washed. A parent should pamper their kids all they want. But there is a limit and a balance. They also should understand that there is a price tag for everything. Jessica's price tag was that she had to live with us, go to school, and learn how to be a productive citizen and adult later in life. It was an example I tried to set for her.

As a child, she had four to five horses. She got a brand new car when she was 16, but she also had good grades and never did anything wrong except cut her hair on her own. She ended up looking like one of the Road Warriors. She never got kicked out of school, drank alcohol, or took drugs. I never had to go to go to the school because she was in trouble, and I never had to pick her up at a police station.

So many parents have those problems. It doesn't matter what your kid looks like or how well they do in school. Just ask yourself, "Is he or she a good kid?" That's what it comes down to, and it is about setting an example. Many parents don't even think about what they do affecting their kid. If they're scum, the kid could become scum. If the parent is a foul-mouthed lowlife, that's what the kid has for an example. If there's abuse, that can be repeated as well. Some kids overcome those obstacles and learn from their parents' mistakes. Many do not and just repeat them.

Not only did I try to be an example for Jessica, I was a bit of a stalker and protector as well. I would call her all the time from the road. When I was home for her first day of school, I followed her bus all the way to school on a motor scooter. Imagine that. A guy who rode a mini-wrestling ring in front of 93,000 people at Wrestlemania 3 in the Pontiac

Silverdome putting around with a scooter after his daughter. A weasel on a scooter. At least, my tail didn't drag or get caught in the wheels.

After awhile, Jessica told me, "Dad, do you know what happens when you put a butterfly in your hands and hold it real tight?"

"No."

"The first time you open it, it flies away and it will never come back, but it you leave your hand open as a nest where it can land, it will always be there."

Smart kid. Kids can teach you things, if you let them. Parents get too wrapped up in being an authority figure. You should be an example and someone does have to set the rules. But there is no reason that you can't take advice from your kids. Sometimes, they have a different or better point of view on situations. They look at things with fresh eyes and see things that older people cannot see.

At that young age, Jessica knew how to express how I was smothering her. That's because I was willing to listen and not just ignore her with a "seen, not heard" attitude that existed when I was a kid.

I always had a rule with Jessica when she was younger. I never let her go anyplace alone. You always hear stories about kids who disappear when their parents turned their backs for a few seconds. You just never know what could happen. When she was 12, I let her go into the store to get a loaf of bread while I waited by the front door in my car. She would come back and I would ask her how much everything cost. She said, "$1.98."

I said, "I gave you a five, where's the change?"

"If I go in to get it, I get the change."

"What if I gave you a 20?" I asked.

"You wouldn't have gotten any change."

I had a rule for her and she had a rule for me, I guess. Every time she goes to get me something, she keeps the change. It still goes on to this day.

As she got older, we did the things that teenagers enjoy, like learning to drive, but she was also developing her sense of humor that was frighteningly similar to mine. I think that's important for parents to do. Teach your kids to laugh. Things have gotten so serious in the world today with 9-11 and terrorism. Sometimes, you have to lighten things up a bit. Sometimes, you have to allow your kid to grow up and develop that comedic style, no matter how strange it may seem.

When I first taught her to drive, I took her to River Hills, the country club we used to belong to. There were homes in the country club's property, but no police. It was quiet during the day with all the mothers home, so I figured it was safe to let her drive around there. She was about

14 or 15 at the time. I would just sip my water as calmly as I could while she drove.

We got home. My wife would say, "Where were you?"

"We went rafting," Jessica said.

My wife had no idea what she was talking about, but, with her being like me, I figured it out. I explained it to Cindi, "I think she meant that we were at River Hills and drinking water while on inner tubes."

I also let her drive on our driveway from the house to the tennis courts. I'd tell her to go and she drove past me. I would yell, "Stop," but she wouldn't stop until I said it again. Meanwhile, I'm following her in the car on foot. This went on forever. I would yell, "Stop," but she wouldn't stop until the second time I said it and would make me follow her. She was doing it on purpose, just for laughs. I was completely blown up by the time we were done.

While she loves the theater and pageants, she thankfully never expressed interest in getting in the business. But that doesn't stop her from being a ham.

I have a friend named Petros, who owns a restaurant in Greektown in Chicago. Cindi, Jessica, and I were there on the afternoon of the Fourth of July. It was nice because not too many people were there. There was Greek music playing in the background and a big stage off to the side. While Cindi and I were talking to Petros, Jessica was walking around the restaurant, pretending she was a waitress, clearing tables off and waiting on people.

The next thing I knew, there were people clapping and there was Jessica Greek dancing on the stage. She immediately went from server to entertainer without missing a beat. The funny thing was that she didn't know how to Greek dance, or so I thought. She just entertained the people.

I took her to a modeling agency when she was four. I told her that she had to be very polite and proper while we were there. I should have known better. When we got to the office, Jessica walked down the aisle, past all the parents sitting there with her kids. She got right up on the desk, sat down, and looked at the person sitting behind the desk, saying, "My name is Jessica, and I'm here to work. Got anything for me?"

She did end up doing some commercials for Minnegasco, Donaldson's department store, and, yes, even the WWF.

She ended up not liking commercials so much, because she had to do things over and over again. She preferred modeling, because you got to wear different clothes and walk down a ramp. There was no repetition, but plenty of attention. Like I said, she likes being a ham like her old man.

She was in a couple of vignettes for WWF television. Monsoon and I were at Busch Gardens, wearing pith helmets and everything else you would have on for a safari. Cindi and Jessica played a woman and her daughter who happened to be walking by. "Aren't you Gorilla Monsoon?" Jessica asked Gorilla.

"Yes," Monsoon said. "How are you?"

She said, "Fine."

Jessica looked up at me and said, "You are a weasel," and stomped my foot. She stomped hard, too. I think she enjoyed it a little too much.

I often brought Jessica to television tapings with me and she even got the opportunity to play a part on WWF TV. She was sitting in the crowd for a television taping and Big Bully Busick walked out for a match. He saw the balloon she was holding, popped it with his lit cigar, and Jessica cried, just like she was told to do. It was all set up in advance. Vince McMahon had told one of his agents to give her 50 bucks for doing it. Jessica came backstage after she was done and the agent handed her 50 dollars. She was beside herself. She had 50 bucks in her hand. For an 11 year old, that's a lot of money.

The next night, the Bully was going to do something else to a kid. I suggested Jessica again and thought of an idea where he would dump Jessica's popcorn on her. Jessica was out there under the lights with all the attention yet again. The popcorn was dumped on her head and she cried. Again, she walked backstage after it was over, but this time there was no agent there and, more importantly, no 50 bucks. I knew she wasn't happy about that.

When I was working and would bring her with me, the rule was that when she was backstage, she stayed in the make-up room. She had fun and got to play with all the wrestlers, including Shawn Michaels and the Undertaker. I came back to the make-up room from taping something and she wasn't there. I started checking dressing rooms to see where she was. Finally, I came to Vince's dressing room, hoping she didn't find her way to his office. I opened the door and there was Jessica. Her hand was out to Vince McMahon.

"You owe me 50 bucks," she said to my boss. I thought I was fired.

Thankfully, Vince was laughing and he reached in his pocket and gave Jessica her payoff.

We left his dressing room, walked around the corner, and I said, "Come here. What were you in there for? Why did you do that?"

"Well, I got paid last night," she said. "There was no agent standing there when I got backstage, so I went to Vince McMahon. I wanted my 50 bucks."

The funny thing is I was on salary, and I never got paid for television. She made more than I did and wouldn't loan me a nickel.

Word got out around the WWF of what Jessica did. Gorilla Monsoon told me, "My contract is almost up. I'm going to have Jessica go in and negotiate for me."

You have to be devoted to your kids, no matter what age they are. They're still your children. Maybe I was overly devoted to Jessica. Maybe I did spoil her, but she respects her mother and father and people overall. We always talked to one another. And by talking, I mean really talking and not yelling. She turned out just fine. Jessica has a college education and works at a bank. She picked a good man as a husband, and they are happy and have been married for two years.

She married a wonderful guy named John. When they got married, I gave them a pair of boxing trunks that was given to me by Joe Louis. It was encased in glass with a little plaque that said, "Presented to Bobby Heenan by Joe Louis at the Checker Dome in St. Louis in 1969." I refer to it in the past tense because my son-in-law hung it up with thumbtacks, which he does with everything. Of course, it fell and it broke. But I love him.

I asked my daughter why she married him. She said, "He reminds me of you."

Like I've always said, "The Brain" thing is only a gimmick for me and apparently it is for my son-in-law too.

Jessica and John got married at a big hotel on the beach of St. Petersburg where Al Capone used to live during the '20s. She actually had her ceremony on the beach. We had an old family friend who took a test to become a notary public just so she could marry them. During the ceremony, I stood behind her. When she would start crying, she would hold out her hand behind her. I thought she was hitting me up for 50 bucks. No, I was carrying Kleenexes for her. In the vows, I would not allow them to write whom I was "giving away." I don't give away, I share. That's how I feel and that's how we wrote it.

There was even a woman playing the harp. I walked up to her and asked, "So, how much do one of those cheese cutters cost?"

She ignored me. I even bumped the strings of the harp, and she wouldn't put me over.

Jessica and John received nice wedding gifts, even one from Vince McMahon himself. He sent a beautiful piece of hand-cut glass. It even had the WWE logo with "Our next pay-per-view is…" inscribed at the bottom. I'm kidding. It's funny. At first it bothered me when I didn't get a call from Vince while I was sick, but when you're as busy as he is, I can see that slipping through the cracks. But he did take time to think of my daughter and, to me, that means as much as anything. I have spoken to him since and I know he wishes me continued good health. I talked to him before this book came out and some of the pictures you see in the photo insert are WWE copyrighted photos that he allowed us to use. That means a lot, since WWE doesn't see a dime for this book. It makes me look back on our working relationship with great fondness. No matter what, I'm his friend, and he'll always be mine.

Meanwhile, Jessica's focus right now is to have a family and kids in a big house. I know she will be as devoted to her children as I was to her. I tried to set that example and show her how important she was to me and continues to be this day.

CHAPTER 13

Cancer, The Ultimate Heel

I asked Mad Dog Vachon once, "How do you want to die, Maurice?" I didn't think he would say in his sleep. That was too nice and calm for a man who was a maniac in and outside of the ring.

He looked at me, smiled, and said, "I don't know, but I wouldn't mind taking someone with me."

The tumor the doctors discovered a few years ago was not the first one I had. I was born with Pyloric Stenosis. I was three weeks premature and weighed nine pounds and eight ounces. My mother thought she was going to have either triplets or a goat. What made me weigh so much is that a tumor had grown in my stomach wall. After I was born, everything I ate, I would throw up. A month later, I weighed four pounds. They took me to Wesley Memorial Hospital in Chicago and operated on me to remove the benign growth. It's a common thing and it certainly isn't fatal. I still carry the scar from that operation that looks like a zipper.

My first experience with cancer was when my aunt died from the disease. But before she died, she cared for her husband, who suffered from Myasthenia Gravis, a neuromuscular disorder. She would have to tape a bell to one of his fingers so when he rang it, she knew he wanted something. She took care of him for a long time before he finally passed away. After that, she went into his bedroom for a year after that and sat there in the dark, staring at the slippers on the floor and crying. She

"There is nothing quite like a good blind referee, except for a rich mother-in-law who likes to go bungee-jumping with a chainsaw."

would have given anything to hear that bell again, no matter how hard it was on her to care for him.

My uncle was never coming back. It didn't do any good for her to pause her life for that entire year. I watched that as a kid. I also watched as she became sicker and sicker with breast cancer. It was very hard, and I saw how she reacted to the pain and the effects of the medication.

The breast they removed was four times the size of an average breast and it was full of veins. It was so hard that you could literally knock on it. After her mastectomy, they treated her with nitrogen mustard, an experimental drug. Her skin was burnt and she lost her hair. She would hallucinate that people were jumping in and out of walls. She was in so much pain and sometimes she couldn't breathe. We had to take her to the hospital every day and the nurses would put a 10-inch needle right under her arm to pull the fluid out. That would allow her to breathe until the next day, maybe two. But I guarantee you, we were there at least five times a week. The difficult thing was that we didn't have the money for that kind of medical service, but our neighbor was the executive director of the Little Red Door Cancer Society. He arranged it so we could have ambulatory service for my aunt.

Finally, my aunt died. All that suffering was finally over for her.

That's why when I got sick, I tried to laugh about things and keep my sense of humor, even throughout my cancer treatments. Medical science has advanced since then. I didn't have to go through what my aunt went through with all the agony and pain, losing her hair, and having a syringe filled with Demerol shoved in her by a boy probably too young to do it.

I counted my blessings while I was sick. I wasn't hooked up to tubes not knowing why my family was crying. I would have hated to see my mother die hooked up to a machine. Or to be a parent and see a young child suffering from cancer before he or she could even take a first step. The kids I saw in the cancer wards hadn't even had a chance to live their lives yet.

Nobody needs to feel sorry for me. I've been to an all-night gas station and I've gotten my face slapped in the back seat of a car. I've had the opportunity to run from angry parents protecting the virtue of their daughter. Some of these kids battling cancer have never played ball or thrown a ball. They've never had a crush or been embarrassed when a girl kissed them. They've never been to a dance. They may not grow up just so they can be kids. I don't know why. It's not fair. They say life's not fair. Well, what's the alternative or answer to that? I say death isn't fair. Life seems to be the only fair thing we have right now.

All those kids in the Ronald McDonald House and the doctors, nurses, and staff that work in those terminally ill units are special people. I can't stand in line in a hotel and if that's the worst thing I'm going through, I can live with it. That's the key word—live. These people work with kids who have serious problems and could die tomorrow.

That patience and compassion that they must have to do what they do inspires me to have a tremendous amount of compassion and respect for them. My hat goes off to them. If you want to pray to whatever god you worship, pray for that kind of patience and the continued care of those who need it. I don't have that kind of patience, and I wish I did. They probably don't make a lot of money doing that, either. I couldn't do their job. I would be a mental wreck to be around that much sickness and death all the time, and I wouldn't know how to handle it.

I love kids and I love the elderly, I always have. Cancer didn't change that so much. I've always had special feelings for children, because of my daughter, my friends' children, and my goddaughter. I would love to be around kids all the time. What I could do is be the guy who runs the merry-go-round. I could be outdoors and enjoy the weather if it is nice and sunny. The kids would be around laughing and having fun.

I love older people from my experiences growing up with my aunt and grandmother. I feel sorry for the elderly, because a lot of people think they are just on their way out and push them aside. Believe me, when you get sick like I did and go through the operations I've experienced on my hip, neck, and knees, you wish for another 25 years, if you can get around. I live in a two-story townhouse and I don't know if I'll be able to go up and down those stairs in another five years.

Yes, older people can be cranky and mean and smell like bad milk sometimes, but God willing, we all will. I know this from my experience living in Florida where there is a high elderly population where they get irritable and mad and won't get out of your way. They feel that they have it coming. They feel they deserve it and will take their time. They will put their money in their purse or wallet at the checkout counter as slow as they feel like it.

You know something. They have a right to it. They survived this long, so let them take their sweet time. Now, before I had cancer, I might have taken a few pokes at granny at the checkout counter. Now, I see it. I'm getting there too. Hopefully, we'll all get there.

You don't think about those things when you're young. You don't think about slowing down and not being able to do the things you once were able to do. You don't think about losing the ones you love and the struggle you go through while they're dying.

Some people get to a point in life where they don't seem to care about their mother and father. They move out of state and don't call. Communication and any relationship completely break down. Sometimes it is too late to repair a relationship and go back to the way things were. Illness can come out of nowhere. Trust me, I know that.

Some don't like to visit anyone—let alone loved ones—in hospitals. A lot of people don't like hospitals. And on behalf of those who have spent time as a patient in a hospital, we don't care if you don't like it. I don't like shaving my neck, but I have to do it. I don't like wiping my ass, but it has to be done. The people in the hospital don't like it either. Go see them and make them feel better. Sacrifice your fear and your pain, take a half hour out of your day, and go visit them. If you're uncomfortable, tough.

In the end, the way to live your life is to be nice to people who are nice to you. Don't be worried about yourself so much. There's a nice way to do things and a wrong way to do things. Be determined to do the right thing.

I was determined to survive from the first day I was diagnosed with cancer in December of 2001. I focused on the fact that I had a beautiful and intelligent daughter, family, and friends, and there are things that I still want to do in life. I'm not suffering today, so I'm not going to be down about it. I look at it like I have the measles or mumps, just a bigger, worse case of it. I hope all the effects of it go away, and the cancer never returns.

Cancer returned for my wife, Cindi. She was diagnosed with breast cancer twice in five years. We made a pact while we were both sick. We were not going to be sad, nor were we going to depress our kid and the people who love us. I don't want to turn the pages ahead and see in the future six months, a year, or five years. There was a time in my life when I would have loved to do that, but not now. Now, I take things day to day and enjoy life. I'm not going to worry about things. What's going to happen will happen. I don't know what the greater power is. Is it God, Allah, or Wally Karbo? What happens will happen.

My cancer was a horrible thing and still remains that way. The doctors told me that even if I recover from it and am completely free from it, I could get it again in a day. It can move all through my body at a moment's notice and at a deadly rate. I know that I could go back to the doctor tomorrow and be given a grim diagnosis. There's always a danger of it coming back, and that is something that I face every day.

But with humor, I will battle it. Not humor at someone else's expense, but humor that makes each day better, no matter what situation I find myself or someone else in. There's no right or wrong way to face possible tragedy. I live with it by telling jokes about it. My wife has had breast cancer twice and I often ask her, "How are you doing?"

She says, "Fine."

I say, "Well, keep me abreast of things."

I laugh about tragedy because I honestly don't like to think about it. I prefer plotting my next practical joke, not how I'm going to get through the day after chemotherapy and radiation treatments. That's my mask. That's my kayfabe.

I make jokes about it and I think that's healthy to do. I'm not making light of things. I'm just trying to make life a little better for me and anyone else who wants to be entertained. We can't be a people or a country that when something bad happens, we just stay depressed like my aunt did after her husband died. You have to go on with your life and not suffer to the point where you feel your life is not worth living. Some people say the most gutless thing to do is commit suicide. To me, the hardest thing to do is to take myself out, because, like I've said, I don't think anybody likes me as much as I do. Imagine reaching that point where there's nothing to care about or go on for and do that to yourself.

There's not much you can do when life doesn't go your way. I've handled my cancer with humor, because that's how I not only wanted to handle it, but also the way I was perhaps supposed to handle it. I entertain myself and others. My aunt handled the death of my uncle by sitting in a room all by herself and crying, because that's how she thought she should handle it. Neither is the wrong thing to do, but I do believe my way of handling things is a better and healthier way of doing things. I also think you respect the dead more by celebrating life instead of mourning death.

It hasn't been easy keeping things light. I had my surgery in March of 2002 and I had to go in back in December of that year after I threw my jaw out from having the dry heaves. I had a lot of setbacks and problems. I found it amazing how many people had cures and suggestions for me to get by day by day. They would tell me to do things like drink lamb's milk.

In the title of this chapter, I refer to cancer as the ultimate heel, but it may be worse than that. I don't even really know what to call it. It was easy fighting the Japanese and Germans in World War II because we knew what they looked like. Terrorists are dressed like us and we don't know what they look like. And we don't know what cancer looks like. The symptoms are different for everyone, or there may be no symptoms at all. People should worry about themselves and stay alert as to what is going on. If something doesn't look or feel right, go tell somebody and have a doctor check you out. No one's going to get mad at you, laugh at you, or think any less of you.

While I would prefer to have the world be like it was when I was younger, the past couple of years in this modern world with me recovering from cancer have been very, very good to me. I've realized that I am very fortunate. Physically, cancer has changed my life, and not really for the better. I still have difficulty saying some words, but that's why God gave us fingers. I have a little trouble swallowing and I can't open my mouth very wide to put a sandwich in it. I can't take that big bite of the burger with 50 pounds of lettuce and an ounce of reindeer. It's too tight from the surgery and radiation.

Emotionally and mentally, it has changed my life for the better. I have a new appreciation for humanity and people. I don't get mad at the guy at the stoplight and I don't drive real fast to get anywhere. I enjoy the sunshine and I hate when it rains. Then again, watching it rain is much better than not being able to. I lost 80 pounds and feel better from that. Again, it's certainly better than the alternative—being in an urn or a box.

I'm still alive.

I live by a new philosophy: IHC. I Had Cancer. I know that every day I'll talk a little better and I'll feel a little better. I can eat. I can travel. I can smile. I have hair. I have friends. And I can breathe in and out. I'm okay.

I have convinced myself that this cancer is not going to beat me down. I'm not going to die from this and have my wife, daughter, family, and friends suffer over a loss. I'm not laying down for this heel. I'll continue to do exactly what the doctor tells me and just hope and enjoy every day of life that I can and I have. That's all I can do. Hope. I'm not sure if praying works. A lot of people pray and never get what they pray for. If someone really needs something, why doesn't somebody—maybe God—give it to them? Maybe he's not there. Maybe he's in Miami or something. Or, again, maybe he's Wally Karbo.

I used to be uptight about things because I was only home for a couple days a week or a month. I was uptight about the business. I was uptight that some people were probably making more than I was and I was doing more work than them. I was playing the roles of a wrestler and a manager. I was producing interviews. If somebody didn't show up, I'd put my wrestling gear on and go out there and take the bumps. I did interviews with my men. I was doing Wrestling Challenge and Prime Time Wrestling with Gorilla Monsoon, Saturday Night's Main Event with Vince McMahon, and the pay-per-views with Monsoon and McMahon. I was flying around the world at a hectic pace.

Now, I wake up in the morning and don't worry about making a town. I do what I want to do. I'm retired now, but most of the friends that I have still have jobs and work during the day. My wife is busy during the day at work. There's not much for me to do, but that's okay. I'll go over to Angelo Poffo's to sit by the pool. Crusher's son Larry will come over to have lunch, or I'll have lunch with my daughter whenever I can.

Instead of racing to the plane, rent-a-car, and hotel, I do normal things like any man my age. I go to the store and get kitty litter and cat chow. I'll mess with the guys at Wal-mart. I'll ask where their thermodizers are. They can't figure out what they are, so they just say, "We're out of them."

All the pressure is off me now—the pressure of working with people who did and didn't know what they were doing. They pay you want they want, and they'll send you where they want when they want to. Now, I can go where I want and when I want. I can say what I want when I want and not worry about pissing off a promoter. I don't have to be at an arena all day long. Even the pressure of waiting in line for security at the airport is gone, which I probably shouldn't mind so much. I believe that they should strip search everybody. In fact, I think it would be great to have everyone walk around the airport naked with their luggage. You'd never see people dropping anything.

Honestly, it wasn't all that bad. The happiest part of the business is when I was in the ring, because I knew who I was in there with. If I didn't like him, I didn't have to do much. It's much better when you like your "opponent," like Pepper Gomez—I loved working with him—or the Crusher. I had fun and laughed and avoided the promoters yelling and screaming. On the other hand, sometimes, I had the Ultimate Warrior, who didn't know what he was doing and could have broken my neck. Not purposely, mind you, but clumsily. Does it really matter how it happened if you are walking around with a broken neck? Then again, I could have broken my neck working at 7-Eleven. I'm married to an Italian woman and her family could have done it.

You just can't worry about things you can't control. You don't know how much time you have. I'm glad to have almost 60 years and done some of the things I did. I'm ashamed of a lot of the things I did too, like talking mean to people at airports and at the building. Cussing and swearing at people. You have to understand that my mentality back then was that I had to be a heel all the time and I had to make the fans hate me no matter what. It was easy to forget that these people were working 40 hours a week, scraping enough money together so they could come and see me. Their hard-earned money allowed me to live in a big home and drive a Mercedes and then turn around and tell them to stick their head up their ass. Looking at it now, it doesn't make sense.

Friends became more special to me as well. Even people who I didn't really consider friends became friends when they took the time to see how I was doing. When I was sick, I had people call me who I would have never dreamed would call me. Kamala e-mailed me. Slick called me and said, "Bobby, you've always been nice to me and you tried to help me. I heard you are having a rough time and wanted to wish you well." He is a reverend with a church in Dallas, and he is a good man. That was amazing that I heard from him. Not because we didn't like each other, but we really didn't have a relationship where we talked all that much outside of the locker room and the arena.

I never worked for Bill Watts, but he called me. Monsoon's wife, Harley Race, and Blackjack Lanza called too. I wish I could name everyone, but, remember, the "Brain" thing is just a gimmick. Angelo Mosca drove from Canada to Florida with his wife. He must have really wanted to see me and really love his wife to drive 1,600 miles with his wife in his car.

It's like the old joke where a guy is driving down the road. The cop pulls him over and says, "Sir, your wife fell out of the car 10 miles back."

The guy says, "Oh, thank God. I thought I went deaf."

Another guy was being chased by a cop for about 20 miles. Finally, the cop gets him to stop and says, "What are you doing? You only have a tail light out."

The guy said, "Oh, I'm sorry. My wife ran off with a state trooper about five years ago. I thought they were bringing her back."

You see, humor can be the best medicine. Laugh at tragedy. Mock adversity. Don't put over the ultimate heel.

If I look back upon things, I wish the wrestling fans and media would have respected us more as actors. On the other hand, I wish we could have been more honest about what we were doing. Right now, all I can do is try to be a better person around the people I care about and even those I don't care about for the days I'm here. I try not to get mad and I don't like to get mad.

I'm happier now. Now I can see my daughter and my friends more. Now I'm free to write this book and do a few independent shows. I answer to no one except my family. The only reason I answer to them is because they deserve that much. If my family wants me to do something, I'll do it even if I don't want to. Just tell me when.

I think I'm more relaxed now after battling cancer. The pressure of traveling, not knowing when you're getting home, and the money not being what you thought it would be has vanished. I wish I didn't have to think about the money I was going to make, but it weighs on my mind constantly. Most people don't worry about what they're going to make because they already know. The only people who didn't know what they were going to make were me and Trixie.

As far as my future in wrestling, I think the business has passed me by. After I left WCW in 2000, I called Vince McMahon at home. He asked me how I was feeling. I told him I was fine and said, "As you probably know, WCW is not going to renew my contract." Vince said, "Well, I'll get with Kevin Dunn. Call me back tomorrow." I tried Vince the next day and couldn't get through to him, so I called Kevin Dunn, who told me to call back in March. I spoke to Kevin in March and he asked if I would be interested in working in Houston at Wrestlemania. I announced the gimmick battle royal and did some autograph sessions.

I received a check and a nice letter from Kevin. That's about the time when I knew something was wrong with me. I didn't know what I had. But I was more occupied by thinking that wrestling was not the same business I once knew. When I went back to the WWF for that one night, I was in the dressing room with all the guys I worked with and I knew very well. I knew the other guys, too, and I watched them shooting routines and scenes. Vince had professional writers handling those things, and it was all different for me. It just didn't seem to be as much fun.

If Vince ever called me for a job, I would say yes if he gave me insurance and I worked one day a week. I don't want to manage or wrestle or any of the fictitious things I used to do. I would love to be a goodwill ambassador and go to conventions and meet-and-greets. I love talking to people and making them laugh. Signing autographs and answering questions never bothered me. I used to act like it did, because I thought I had to act that way.

But the pressure may return. The pressure of having to go where they would want to send me. I don't know if I want to do that anymore. I never say never, but I've been told what to do since I was born and all the way through my career in the wrestling business. I was told where to wrestle, who to wrestle, and taking the money they wanted to give me, not necessarily what I earned. Now, I don't have to go anyplace if I don't want. I can give myself what I want. If the money is right, I'll do it. If it's not, I won't do it. No hard feelings.

I was flattered when WWE asked me to do Confidential. Plus, they let me plug my first book when they didn't have to do that, and I thought it was very nice of Vince to allow that. I don't know why he did it. When I was there, we could never mention another brand or product. Maybe it was the years I've been in business. Gene Okerlund called me to see if I wanted to do the show. They came out and shot some footage.

Some people from the *WWE Magazine* also came over to my house for a photo shoot for *Raw Magazine*.

I never thought I would get to this point. I never used to see how the oldtimers just refused to watch wrestling anymore. How could they not watch it? It was their life. But I don't think I want to be a part of it anymore. There are people I don't know. It's other people flying around in their underwear. I know some of the guys, but it's not the same. I lost interest in that. I have developed other interests.

I don't even want to visit backstage, because everyone thinks you're there looking for a job if you hang around. If I'm going to a wrestling event, I want to be paid for it. It's business. I don't really know if I could rekindle my juices for it.

If I went back, they might try to talk me into taking bumps again, and I'd probably do it. I just want to enjoy my life. I could live to be 100. That's a long time I would have to enjoy life.

There is no pressure in not working for WWE. The scariest thing in my life nowadays is not that I won't have a job with WWE. It's the unknown. The pressure I felt when I left WCW was that I would eventually lose the insurance never having it before my time there. I really didn't want to go back to that, but I didn't know how to get insurance. I was waiting for Vince to call, but I never had insurance when I worked for him anyway. If I went back full-time, I would have to ask to be an employee again and have insurance. I had to ask myself if I even wanted to go back and travel four to five days a week. Even if I only worked three days a week, I would have to leave a day before and a day after. I'm almost 60, and I have to ask myself, "Do I want to do that anymore?" No, I don't. But I felt I had to if I wanted insurance.

In the end, my wife offered to get a job. No one would hire me. I have no skills. I can read. I can spell, except for really big words. If I have to write, "You're ludicrous," I write, "You're the shits." I know how to get around it. It's pretty much the same meaning anyway.

She found a job that pays hardly anything. It's sad because we had already given up being members of a country club. It wasn't so much for financial reasons as much as we just didn't play golf anymore. We still live well. We have a Mercedes and a Lexus and live in a townhouse on the beach. Everything is fine except our health, which, if you think about it, is fine. We're alive and feeling a little better every day.

My first book couldn't have come along at a better time. We sold beyond all expectations and had people showing up at bookstores for signings. I knew I was a different kind of product, because I've been on television for so long. We were at malls with long lines and sold out all the books to be signed. I remember in Milwaukee, there was a mix-up in the publicity and there was no advertising for the event. We still drew what we normally drew in other cities where there was some marketing. Even being on the south side of Chicago on Labor Day, we still had a heck of a crowd.

That surprised me. I guess wrestling is a lot more popular than people think it is. Actually, Nitro was outdrawing the Braves on TNT. I signed everything, too, no matter what the bookstore manager or the publisher wanted me to do. It takes longer to say, "Get lost," and, "No" than it does to sign the cover of a wrestling magazine.

But I found it funny what fans will remember. One came up to me and said, "My brother told me that he spit on you and threw a beer at you in St. Paul. Then, he swung at you and missed you, so you body-slammed him."

"He's lying to you," I told him.

"No."

"Why would I do that? Why didn't he call the police if I body-slammed him."

"He didn't care."

"Have you ever been in a fight?"

"Yes," he said.

"You don't bodyslam somebody. You go for his nuts," I explained to him.

That's the best advice in a fight. Go for the round things. If he's got you up, get his eyes. If he's got you down, go for his balls.

In the end, I'm like every other man. I get tired every night. We all do and that's why we all go to bed. I want to get better and get as close as I can to being healthy. I've done everything in the wrestling business, except wrestle a woman. I don't want to wrestle a woman or anyone for that matter. I've wrestled a midget and wrestled a bear. That's enough for one life.

I do worry about passing away. I am scared of making my daughter, my wife, and my friends unhappy. I don't ever want to hurt anyone. That's what concerns me. I'm afraid of dying—everyone is—but I accept it and whatever comes after death. There's no way out of it. Like W.C. Fields said when he was reading the Bible, "I'm not religious. I'm just checking for loopholes."

Before I had cancer, I only worried about my family passing away. Now that I have cancer, I don't want to hurt them.

You don't need cancer to change your viewpoint. When you see all the terrorism and what goes on in the world, you learn to appreciate life. It could all end tomorrow. You don't have to let a life-threatening illness change your life. Look at your life while you have the opportunity. Look at it with clear eyes, not eyes filled with tears while suffering from tragedy, whether it's your own or someone close to you. Look forward and focus on how you can improve your life. Don't look back and see ways you could have changed.

Be kind to the people you love and cherish your children. There's not much more you need to do. You don't need religion or psychic hot-lines. Don't keep thinking that you need something. As long as you have yourself and your loved ones, you're fine, unless you're a part of the family with the kid on the porch from Deliverance.

In dealing with the ultimate heel called cancer, my thinking is that I didn't do anything to keep from getting it, I'm not sure what I did that made me get it, and I don't know how to get rid of it. I'd have to do the best I can to get rid of it again. Because I'm a manager, not a wrestler. But then again, I'm really not a manager. You know, maybe I never had cancer. Maybe they lied to me and it was all a work. Maybe it was lumbago. I don't know. That's the reality or lack of reality I've always lived with.

In the end, the ultimate heel turned this career heel into the ultimate babyface.

CHAPTER 14

Life's Heels, Naysayers, Enemies, and Pests...
What We Can Learn from Them

S ometimes you wouldn't get checks for months. Then, the promoters would get mad at you if you called and asked where your money was. I remember in St. Louis, I would get preliminary match money all the time, no matter where I was on the card. I asked Bruiser, "How come I get $125 to $250 and the guy I'm managing is making $1,200 to $1,500?"

Dick would say, "But, Bobby, you're the first manager in the history of the NWA to manage in St. Louis."

I said, "Well, thank you, Dick. Next time I'm in Kroger's and I buy $50 worth of groceries, and they ask me for the money, I'm going to say, 'Whoa, I'm the first manager in the NWA in St. Louis. Now would you please bag up my groceries and show me the door so I can get home?'"

Baron Von Raschke once told me that 90 percent of people are pretty good guys. The other 10 percent are jerks. To me, he is the epitome

"If a guy sticks his hand out to you, shake it...and then kick him real hard when he's not looking."

of a fine and upstanding human being, and I told him that he was probably a little bit off, but he can never see the dark side of life. He is too nice a man. There are nice people in the business, but the majority are not. This is a cash business—a money business. This is just the way it is.

If you get hurt and you can't work anymore, you're of no use to your boss. But remember that you're not given that job as a favor to make you money. Your boss is doing it to make himself money. If you're making money along the way and he's not losing any, that's fine for him.

It's like people saying, "Boy I got a deal today." The commercials tell you, "Boy, have I got a deal for you." You know what a deal is? A deal is something you want, not what the other guy is willing to give. No one is going to really offer you a true deal. No one is going to sell you a car for $100 when they paid $150, just because they like you. They sell it to you because they don't want to pay for it anymore or can't pay for it and want to get out of it while they can. Remember, the guy selling it doesn't want it. He didn't want to get rid of it for nothing, and if he didn't want to get rid of it, there'd be no deal. That's the way life is. People will only give you what they want to give you.

People can be so gullible. You can sell anything to anyone. Freddie Blassie was a salesman's dream and bought more gimmicks than anyone. He just loved owning them, whether he was being ripped off or not.

When my grandfather owned his haberdasher, his philosophy was that the customer had to be right because you were dealing with the people in the neighborhood. I guarantee you that the customers he had were the customers who were loyal to him for a long time. He rarely had new ones. If he had 50 customers, that was his customer base.

That kind of loyalty is rare. But the business owners only have themselves to blame, because caring about service and product quality is a thing of the past. Look at fast food restaurants nowadays. I guarantee you that there is more food in my teeth right now as I write this book than there are in their burgers. They talk about so many billions of hamburgers that they have served. That almost equals one pound of meat. You see these burgers on their commercials with grease dripping down someone's arm. Lift the bun when you get it. It looks like one of those five-day deodorant pads—used.

Service is not what it used to be. I was staying at a hotel in Minnesota while working on this book. I called down to room service because I had to take my cancer medication and couldn't do it on an empty stomach. I just wanted to have lunch at 1:00, nothing more. I ordered some walleye fingers. Only in Minnesota. Walleyes don't have fingers. Then again, buffalos don't have wings. Now, wine comes in a box and booze comes in plastic bottles. The number-one rapper is white. The number-one golfer is black. And the tallest guy in the NBA is Chinese. Who booked that one? It makes no sense. It's just like what Charles Manson once said, "No sense makes sense."

But I digress. So I called down to room service to order my food a little after one. The woman on the phone told me that the kitchen was closed. I hung up, disappointed that I wouldn't get my hands on those walleye fingers, so to speak. But I started thinking about it and what that lady told me just didn't sound right. Sure enough, I looked at the menu and it said that lunch is served until 1:30 in the afternoon. I called her back, and she had the nerve to say, "That's a misprint." Before I could respond, she continued, "There's nothing I can do about it." I was about ready to tell her what she could do or where she could put those walleye fingers—all 10 of them, one at a time.

I decided to call the general manager of the hotel. "You know, I don't want to be a pain in the ass," I told him. "But, damn it, what would you do if they advertise the Super Bowl at a certain time and it started at a different time?"

I pleaded my case and the manager agreed with me. Sometimes, I just get tired of being advertised something and not getting what is promised. "Was she rude to you?" he asked.

"No," I answered. "But she clearly didn't care."

It seems that no one in "customer service" really cares about the customer anymore. Probably because of the constant turnover in customers already. But if that hotel had only 50 extremely loyal and regular customers like my grandfather had, they would be having lunch all day long.

Hotels were easy to hate. For some, it was hard to check in and check out or their computers were always down. And even if they guaranteed a room, by the time I arrived, it would be given away. It seemed like they were double-booking rooms to make more money.

No matter how small it may seem, there are things that happen in this world that prove that those in customer service simply don't care about you. Why do you have to go through the aisle that requires 11 items or less and the guy in front of you has 12 and they won't send him away? Can't they count? They're running a cash register, for crying out loud.

Some people are jerks for the sake of being jerks, and there is nothing you can do to change them. But there are things you can do when dealing with them. Those types of heels come in all shapes and sizes. Heels don't just show up in wrestling rings. They show up in all aspects of life. The idea is to recognize them, deal with them, and learn from them. Fight fire with fire, I say. An unreasonable situation sometimes causes you to act unreasonably as well. Sometimes, it's the only language that some people understand.

I was in Chicago one night and it was really cold—probably below zero. I swear that wind chill causes brain damage. There was this island that I had to stand on outside to wait for a cab. When I would finally find a cab driver, I would ask him to take me to the nearby Marriott O'Hare. "Take the bus," he would say to me. That was unfair, and the more I experienced that, the more I learned that telling them exactly where I wanted to go wasn't going to get me to the place I wanted to be.

I would have to convince him it was an emergency and I promised him a good tip for the short trip that wasn't worth his time. When we would get to the hotel, I would pay the fare, but nothing more. He would ask, "Where's the tip?" I would tell him, "Here's your tip. Don't believe everything you hear."

The same thing would happen in Toronto, plus it took forever to get through customs before you could even try to find a cab, which made it later and colder. The cab drivers would never want to take you short distances because they would have to get out of the line in front of the airport and the fare wasn't worth it to them. I needed to get to my hotel. That was my objective and the cab was the only way to get there. I wasn't going to walk. So I would tell the driver to take me to the York Hotel, which was a fancy place about an hour from the airport. Less than a mile into our trip, I would tell the driver to make a quick stop at the Howard Johnson's so I could talk to a buddy who was in town. I'd go into that hotel, wait a minute or so, and then come out and say that I've decided to stay with my friend after all.

While I loved to mess with the cab drivers, it shouldn't have come down to that. They should have just taken me where I wanted to go because it's what they're supposed to do. It's not my fault that they don't like their jobs or couldn't get better ones. But, there was no convincing them. While I had to deceive the drivers, I didn't cheat them out of their fares. They didn't get a big tip or any tip for that matter, but they didn't deserve it.

Take funeral directors, for example. No really, take them please. You would think that they would care about you more. You're in their business when you're at your most vulnerable and they can charge you anything. After my mother died, I went to a funeral director whose last name—I swear—was Die and he looked exactly like Vincent Price with his hair combed back and a pencil-thin mustache. He had a white-on-white shirt with a cream tie and a pinstriped black suit and cufflinks. When he touched me, his hands were cold and very white. He smelled like carnations. If all that wasn't bad enough, his assistant was named Mr. St. Pierre—like St. Peter.

He took me down to the basement to select the casket. It was a showroom similar to what you would see at a car dealership. He showed me the first casket for around $500. I didn't like it, so I asked him what was the next step up. He showed me one that had to cost $12 million. It was lead lined and airtight. I ended up picking something that I thought would be nice for my mother. He suggested a dress for my mother. She always wore housedresses, so I wanted her to have a nice dress. He took one out and laid it in the casket, "What do you think?"

It looked great on the casket.

Then he asked me, "Would you like some panty hose with it?"

Now I was getting mad, "Hey, where the hell is she going? You can rip the ass out of the dress, I don't care. She's not leaving the box, pal."

I swear he was going to suggest some pumps and a purse to go with the dress and the casket.

Even going through the airport is different. They don't let you bring a nail clipper on board any more. What am I going to do with that but cut my own nails? Anyone can bring a mirror on board, smash it, and they have a piece of sharp glass—an instant weapon. But a nail clipper? I can hear the passengers now, "Oh my God, he's got a nail clipper and he's going to trim! Put your shoes on, Harry!"

And they give you drinks on the plane. That never made sense to me. They check you for weapons before you get on the plane and once you're there, they give you all the booze you want and a plastic knife with your meal.

In my life, I have learned something. I don't write letters to people because I never see them get it. I don't see their reaction. I don't see if they even throw in the garbage. But that shouldn't stop you if you really feel the need to complain about life's heels. Be direct and vent. It may not help you a great deal in getting things the way you want them, but it will keep you off the rooftops with a high-powered rifle.

In this world, the hardest type of person to trust is a politician who says one thing and does another. Sounds like the heel that I used to portray. I think that the image of politicians was tarnished with Richard Nixon. Others before him may have been crooked and forced from office, but he held the highest elected position. Franklin Delano Roosevelt was the president when I was born. I knew nothing of him but heard he was a great man. Then again, I also heard he had a mistress, so you never can tell.

Watch carefully when a politician leaps into a crowd of people and not just to protect your wallet. He'll extend the ol' paw, but never look at anyone in the face. All they're doing is just trying to get another vote. Once somebody gets elected, they don't seem to care unless they're up for re-election.

They have to watch what they say when they're running for office. Some politicians don't want to say that they'll cut welfare, because the people on welfare will vote against them. Some take strong stands on certain issues, but their supporters can never count on them staying true to what they said. If I was running for office and welfare was an issue, I would propose that everyone could have welfare if they have had a job for 10 years and paid their income tax. For one year, the government should provide an income and that's it. You're done for 10 years and you need to get a job.

I don't care how many kids someone has, either. Just because you're unemployed and have nine kids does not qualify you for welfare. I could steal enough money to buy rubbers.

The problem is that the welfare system has so many abusing it, and it's not just one race, either, in spite of what others would have you believe. Don't get me wrong. A lot of people need welfare. A lot of people need help. But you have to earn that help. Work and pay your taxes. People don't want to work anymore. They seem to be too lazy to work. It is hard to respect those kinds of people.

Don't forget, there are more people being born than dying. We're getting overpopulated, and the world is constantly changing. I've been around for 59 years and I've seen so much change in this world, so much change in the past two years since I had cancer.

When the world is constantly dealing with heels, it creates an atmosphere where everyone is out for himself, and it's only going to get worse. It's going to be more vicious and dog eat dog. My daughter is 25, and I hope she has another 50 years, but her kids are going to be experiencing something completely different.

There was a book out years ago called *The Good Old Days...They Stunk*. Back in those "good" old days, there was no air conditioning. The food tasted different. There were no drive-in restaurants. Fathers wore white shirts and ties and took the family out to church every Sunday. What's different about life now is the people running our lives—the politicians and people in charge of this world—who believe that power is money. And they rip everyone off at their own expense just to push their agenda.

When I was with WCW, we were having a production meeting where we discussed an angle where Bill Goldberg would spear these guys who were actors dressed up in suits and ties to look like attorneys. They were lawyers who forced Goldberg into some situation and the only thing he could do was spear them.

In the meeting, I was sitting there with my "bosses" and the other production people. They presented the angle and then asked if anyone had any questions. I raised my hand and suggested, "If you're going use those guys, have the agents setting up the angle tell them to stay down. If they're working for a law firm and get speared by Goldberg, they shouldn't be able to walk away."

They paused, looked at each other, and then looked at me and said, "Thank you, Bobby." They both seemed insulted that I would suggest something that was against what they wanted.

In the end, Goldberg speared the three "attorneys" and right after it, they jumped back up and left the ring. They did it because they're actors and don't know about wrestling. You have to sell what happens to you, especially when it comes from a monster such as Goldberg. How would fans buy it if WCW didn't sell it?

My goal then and always was to try to better the product that I was associated with. All I wanted to do was help and not hurt it. They were too unprofessional to understand what I was doing. It was as if I suggested something that went against their plan, when actually, they couldn't possibly come up a good idea. They simply weren't creative enough. 83 weeks of Nitro beating Raw, my ass. If you're successful, you stay on top, not brag about how you were on top.

A true heel in life is never all that creative, because they are out for themselves. That limits what they can do and what they are able to do. Remember, the cream doesn't always rise to the top, especially in professional wrestling. The leadership in the WCW weren't the cream. They were the residue. They emptied everything good out of WCW, and they were left to feed off what was on the bottom.

Remember, there are some people in positions of power who have no business being there. Eric Bischoff hired me and paid me, but I still don't think he belongs in this business to this day. I earned every dime I was paid and I don't take charity from anyone. I've earned my money. Even though I'm now 180 pounds and crippled, life's heels will never beat me.

If you want to tell if someone in a position of power knows nothing about the wrestling business, the first thing they do is put themselves on television, turn heel, and become a full-blown manager. They're out of ideas and don't even put over the fact that they are in a booking or creative position. They essentially demote themselves. The only men I knew in the wrestling business who were successful promoters and never worked as wrestlers or managers were Dennis Hilgaard in Milwaukee and Sam Muchnik in St. Louis.

I remember St. Louis most for the rings being so hard. The boys would complain that Sam wouldn't replace that rock-hard ring. I told them that I knew how I could get a new ring. I suggested that every Friday night after the national anthem, someone needed to pull Sam in the ring and bodyslam him. If he had to drop his big ass in the ring four times a month, we'd have a new ring in no time, and a much softer one, too. The boss has to know what it's like for his employees.

Your boss may be your boss, not because you wanted him to be or he was the most talented. He knew what to do and what to say to get where he is. He may have screwed a friend or held others down. Deal with him honestly and you could lose your job.

When I started in Indianapolis, there were two people who helped me break into the business, or I guess "drafted" me into the business. One of the people I really cared about was Wilbur Snyder, a decent, nice man. The other man, Dick the Bruiser, I just pretended to like. Honestly, I despised that man. I pretended to like him because he paid me. I was supporting three people in my household, so I had to like him. If I didn't like him, I'd be back at the Ford dealer, struggling to take care of my family.

I used him to get where I wanted to in life to benefit my family. He used me in return. He would make me do things that I didn't want to do, like run stupid errands to the hardware store when I just wanted to play football with my friends. I was a kid, for Christ's sake, but I couldn't be a kid with him around. I would have to leave a game so I could call him twice a day every day of the week, 10 in the morning and 2 in the afternoon for no reason whatsoever, just to check in. And if he was on the phone, booking a card or something for about an hour, I'd have to wait wherever I was and call him back when the line wasn't busy. If I didn't, he'd get mad at me. And if he got mad at me, he wouldn't pay me and would treat me bad. I needed the money, so I kissed his ass for all those years to make a living.

Right before I left in 1974, Bruiser turned me babyface, but during a match where I tagged with him against The Sheik and his manager, he turned me back heel. He was threatened by the success I had achieved and didn't want a bigger babyface than he was.

And then I finally went to the AWA and worked for Verne Gagne. I no longer needed Dick and never worked for him again. It's sad to say, but that's how I got even with him. I was his number-one star. Two mayors of Indianapolis proclaimed Bobby Heenan days. No wrestler has ever had a day for themselves in Indianapolis, not even Dick the Bruiser. That's how over I was in Indianapolis. More over than he ever was.

Dick never did anything despicable or nasty as much as he was just a demanding person. There were things about him, characteristics about him, and the way he conducted himself with those close to him that I didn't like. I couldn't change it. So I always looked at him as an employer and not a friend, but I pretended to be his friend, because that's what he wanted and he would give me what I really wanted from him. Money. Money to support my family and live my life.

I felt ashamed sometimes. Hell, I felt like a liar and a cheat, but I needed to feed the family. I figured that I wasn't lying and cheating against my mother or anybody I respected or liked. I was doing it to one of my life's heels that I didn't respect or like. He had the check, and I needed to take it.

I hold no animosity toward Dick the Bruiser and his family. It was over and done with in 1974 as far as I was concerned. He told me when I said I was leaving that I'd never make it without him. Well, I went to the AWA, NWA, WWF, and WCW. I made it without him.

But sometimes you have to stand up to the idiots who take up the air we breathe. It's sad to say, but sometimes you have to shut your mouth to fill your stomach. That's what it's all about. You have to do a lot of things in life that you don't like.

When I was 18, I worked at a department store in Indianapolis with this 40-year-old stock boy, a lifetime employee as far as I could see. I was there mostly because I could hide upstairs and see people in the dressing rooms. While that's not something I'm necessarily proud of, it is something that everyone reading this should know—even the deadbeats who didn't buy this—that whenever you're in a dressing room in a store, someone can always watch you.

They put this lifetime stock boy in charge one day and it went right to his head. He paged me and told me to go to the loading dock and unload a truck full of merchandise. I told him I'd get to it, but honestly I was a better flirt than I was a stock boy. I was walking around and talking with girls, pinching them or whatever else I did when I was younger. My stock boy supervisor caught me talking to this girl and yelled, "Get down to the dock."

I said, "Hey, I'm going down there. I'm on my way."

He grabbed me by the shirt and punched me in the mouth right there in the store. The problem was he wasn't powerful enough to hurt anyone. So I shoved him and he fell down. I walked away and went into the waiting room where they tried on wedding gowns. People don't buy wedding gowns every day, so I went in there and locked the door to take a break from my job and this idiot. I kept hearing him paging me over the intercom again. I didn't answer it. At five o'clock, I walked out of the room and punched out for the day.

The boss was there waiting for me. He took me back into his office. "Where have you been all day?" he asked.

"I've been on strike," I told him.

"For what?"

"Jerry punched me in the mouth, and I shoved him. I knew he and you were looking for me for that."

My boss threatened me, "I could fire you right now for that."

"You can fire me because he punched me in the mouth?" I asked.

"Yes."

I leaned over the desk and punched him in the mouth and said, "Now we're both unemployed."

He told me to get the hell out of there. The truth was I knew he liked me and would never fire me no matter what. He didn't.

I wanted to get transferred to their downtown store, which was bigger. They put me in the mailroom with two women, one named Butch. I worked in there all day long. I never saw the store or any customers. From there, they transferred me to the west side of Chicago. But it was a warehouse where you loaded refrigerators and couches all day. I should have stayed back in the first store and punched myself in the mouth.

Ox Baker immediately comes to mind as another idiot in my opinion, not to mention a heel that I had to deal with. That man never knew when to open his mouth or shut it. "Sailor" Art Thomas—who passed away recently—was a friend of mine and a wonderful man. He was an African American in a business where there wasn't a lot of tolerance. I don't think he ever saw the difference between black people, white people, Asian people, or Hispanic people. He would always have a smile for me, and we would always talk about the movies or something like that. He was the kindest, gentlest man there could be. And he was a good wrestler with a great, natural physique. He would never stick himself with a needle.

Art would always come into the dressing room with a nice-looking suit and tie and greet everyone with a smile. On one occasion, Baker saw him come in and immediately started singing, "Mammy's little baby loves shortnin' bread." Some got up and walked out of the room while others stuck around just to see what Art would do to Baker. I know what we all wanted Art to do, but it just wasn't in his nature. I don't know if he was even paying attention to Baker and if it even hurt him if he did hear that moron. Baker had been in the business for many years, and he knew better. He just decided to be an idiot.

I will never forget that. How disrespectful he was to a man who showed nothing but respect. Baker wanted everyone in the dressing room to laugh at Art and laugh with him and his stupid song. I don't know if he intended to hurt Art, but that's not the point. They cured my cancer. There's no cure for Ox Baker. So, if you have cancer, there's hope. If you're stupid, you're stuck with it forever.

Racism is ugly, whether it's what someone believes or just a one-time, stupid comment. Do you think that racists are proud of their beliefs? Then why the hell does the Ku Klux Klan wear hoods? Why do they burn their crosses in the dark of night? Heels come in all races, colors, and creeds, but it doesn't mean that they tolerate all races, colors, and creeds.

Some heels in life are almost so good at what they do, you can't help but admire them. Buddy Rogers—the first WWE (then WWF) champion—was truly one of those heels in life who was a backstabber, but he was so good at it and really smooth. I'm not proud if it, but part of me admired what he did. Anyone would, as long as they were not on the receiving end of what Rogers did. He was smart and knew every back-stabbing way to get himself over in that ring.

Rogers would take the legs of his opponents underneath his arms and give them the giant swing around. But Rogers would add a little twist. He would let go and his opponent would fly over the top rope and into the crowd. After the match, he would tell the guy that he just slipped. And that's how he got over. The poor bastard he sent over the ropes couldn't remember his name if his life depended on it. Goddamn, he was so cool. He got away with it and saved face.

Other wrestlers weren't so smooth at being a heel. In fact, they were insecure. They were the kind of guys who would ask you, "How was my match?" I never asked that, because I knew how it was, and I didn't need someone else to tell me if something was shitty. I was aware if it was good, bad, or just one of those nights. It's like making love to a woman. You don't have to ask the guy across the hall if it was good or bad. You have a pretty good idea.

There was a wrestler named Jerry Blackwell, who was really fat, but a good worker. He was one moody son of a bitch. If he felt like talking to you, he would. If he was pissed off, it was like you didn't exist. I don't like that at all and never have. I can't stand fair weather friends. Talk to me all the time or don't talk to me at all.

Jerry came back from the ring one night. "How was the match?" he asked me.

I said, "Fine."

"You think so?"

"Yeah."

The next night he asked me the same thing, "How was my match?"

I was getting tired of it, so I told him the truth.

"It was the shits," I said.

"Well, what the hell do you know?" he yelled back at me.

Why did he ask me in the first place? To tell you the truth, I never saw the match. I was never out in the arena when I wasn't wrestling or concerning myself with what others were doing. Heels in your life will ask for feedback and not want honesty. They'll butt in with their own feedback when you never asked in the first place. Some people just can't be happy.

For me, when I was making more money than I ever made, I was extremely happy and as nice to people I could be. I was happy making money. But I would always see people fight and argue with anyone over the stupidest things when they weren't making money.

I look at things this way. It's just wrestling. Let's have some fun with it. You don't want to worry about other people's lives and pasts and who is going to stab you in the back. It's too much to worry about. I want the woman at the bank to smile at me and say, "Thank you, Mr. Heenan," when she deposits or cashes my check. And I want to see my wife, daughter, family, and friends enjoy life.

Professional wrestling is the strangest industry in the world. The priorities of the wrestlers are sometimes completely out of whack. Wrestler A would say, "I'm in the main event, and you're not."

Wrestler B would say, "So what?"

Wrestler A then would say, "I had your wife before."

"So what?" says Wrestler B.

Then, Wrestler A would say, "You had a lousy match."

Wrestler B yells, "Oh yeah?" and want to fight you.

A wrestling heel doesn't have to scripted by a booker or television writer. They can be a heel on their own in how they treat other wrestlers and their families. Sometimes their gimmick overtakes them, and they become what they portray in the arena and on television. Work life can overtake anyone. The goal is to find a balance and not let your "heelness" consume you.

There are wrestlers who made things so difficult. They never said "thanks" after a long match. The fun of working—whether in the wrestling ring or in an office—is knowing that you're appreciated and respected by the person you're working with. It's hard to explain to somebody the feeling of having a really good performance in a match. You sure as hell know when you have a bad one. There are some nights you could have a Thompson sub-machine gun aimed at the crowd and you won't get heat.

You could have the best "hand" in the world out there but something will get missed. Or you go out to the arena and there will be no one in the house. Some nights you can hit that high note and other nights you just can't get to it. It's a great feeling to shake the hand of the guy who has been protecting your body for a half hour and ask if he's okay. You brag how you both had the audience in the palms of our hands with one spot and how happy you felt that we planned to put that in there at the right time. That was the fun of working. That can be the fun of collaborating. But instead of just saying "thanks," sometimes all you see is the back of your opponent walking back to the dressing room without saying a goddamn word.

Some guys can't get those two words out of their mouth. It is just proper etiquette to say "thank you" to the guy doing the job and losing the match for you. I said "thank you" even if I was the one doing the job. I thanked the man for not hurting me. I would wrestle Hulk Hogan and while the referee was making that three-count, I'd say, "Thank you, Terry" and he'd thank me back. It's a wonderful feeling to know that you worked with one man and you succeeded. It's sad when that interaction is not there.

Instead of thanking their co-workers, some guys will pick apart their performance. They never quite got it. They didn't realize that the fans in the arena don't know what we're really doing in there, all the communication and subtlety of the match. Why worry about it? We knew the spot that needed to be called, but the fans did not.

Teamwork is the key, and when mistakes are made, that's when teamwork comes into play. When things get tough, a heel will abandon his partner and blame him for everything. A heel will point a finger at the other guy and make trouble instead of finding a solution.

Wrestling has its share of heels who refuse to cooperate and work with anyone in a respectable way. They shoot off their mouth when they should just shut up. Yet, when a "heel" is silent, be careful. He may be plotting to stick a knife in your back.

No one likes to be double-crossed and lied to, because it betrays trust. How do you expect to establish trust when someone says one thing and does another? Whenever fans of professional wrestling think of double-crosses, they think of what happened to Bret Hart at the 1997 Survivor Series in Montreal. Don't get me wrong. I like Bret. He's a nice guy and I've known him and his entire family for years. But if he thought for one moment that Vince McMahon was going to give up complete control over whether he won or lost a championship, he was mistaken. I wouldn't even give anyone complete control, and I'm not Vince McMahon.

Vince had to look out for what was best for his company. He felt that as the owner of the company, he had to make the call whether Bret retained or lost the WWF championship. He thought that putting the belt on Shawn Michaels was the best move for his company. His company and no one else's. Bret didn't want to do it, so McMahon double-crossed him and arranged a different finish to the match.

Bret should have just put Shawn over and not worried about it. He was on his way to WCW anyway, with a big money contract. I understand that he may not have liked Shawn, but he had to understand that he was never going to get one up on the guy who owns the company. Period. If he thought he had control, he only had that control because Vince allowed him to have it. And what Vince giveth, Vince can taketh away.

In the end, Bret never had true control, no matter what a contract may say. None of us ever did. It was just a bad move on his part, but that's his business, and I think everyone has moved on. At least I hope so. We all make decisions in life that we regret, but he's a grown man. I never let that so-called "heel" promoter get to me, because I really never cared if I won or lost. I lived by what Gorilla Monsoon told me and did my job for the money. I never won a title belt in my life. It was just more to carry onto the plane.

So tell me, who was the heel in that situation? Sometimes they're hard to identify. Things are not always black and white. There are shades of gray. Everyone has a story and everyone has an excuse. But trust me, if it looks like a heel, smells like a heel, and acts like a heel, it's a heel.

Everyone still talks about when Vince Russo double-crossed Hogan in the summer of 2000. I was announcing for WCW at the time, but no one ever told us what was going to go down or what would happen after. The people in charge never discussed anything with us. From what I could see, it was just a regular match when Jeff Jarrett laid on the mat, allowing Hogan to pin him.

In all honesty, I didn't care what happened there by that point. Hogan was one of many. Everyone was getting double-crossed in WCW. It was run so poorly. I swear that if Ted Turner was in charge of daily operations, we would have been popping out of cornfields like on *Hee Haw*. I would have eventually been doing commentary with Buck Owens. I just had to keep in mind, "I'm getting benefits. I'm getting benefits."

Wrestling promoters don't just double-cross their employees, they also double-cross their fans or their customer base. They incorporate these wrestling storylines (or angles for you mooching deadbeats) that resemble real life and have little to do the actual in-ring product. It's called a work-shoot.

I guarantee you that there are people to this day who still believe that Owen Hart is still alive and that, back in 1999, WWE presented an angle that he died. It's sad that some fans believe that, but it's even sadder that wrestling promotions have conditioned their fans to not quite buy what's on television. Vince McMahon admitted that wrestling was a staged event, so when real life enters into it, very few will buy it.

I miss Owen. He was from a wrestling family. His brother was Bret Hart and his father was Stu Hart, an old-time wrestler and a promoter. They were all such nice people. Owen had an amazing amount of talent, but someone decided to put a mask on him and have him walk around as the Blue Blazer, a superhero. On the night he died, he was on a catwalk near the roof of the Kemper Arena in Kansas City. He was supposed to "fly" down like a superhero while being hung on an apparatus and land in the ring.

Sting was using the same thing in WCW. Even before Owen died, I would watch Sting do that stunt and be completely terrified for him. I'm scared of heights. I wouldn't even date a girl who wore high-heeled shoes. I guess in a way, I admired Sting and thought he had no fear. I told him that one night and he said, "You should empty my trunks when I'm done." He was scared. Everyone was. And if you weren't, there was something wrong with you.

From what I understand, Owen rehearsed it during the day. When it came time for his introduction, he was hanging there ready to go, but somehow the apparatus failed or he released himself accidentally and plummeted to his death. It was a tragedy to this business to lose someone like that.

I still remember the night it happened. Bob Ryder approached me when I got into town for a Nitro broadcast at 11 p.m. He told me that Owen had died and how he died. I'm rarely speechless and all I could say was, "My God."

A lot of people blamed Vince McMahon for it. First of all, if it was me who had to fall from the rafters, I wouldn't have done it, even if I was threatened with being fired. There are some things that I just cannot do. Owen, like a good employee, kept his mouth shut as the "heels" in his life were maybe making him do something that he didn't want to do. I think he did what he did to keep food on the table, and he should be admired for that. A wrestling angle is certainly not worth dying for.

WWF can come up with ideas, angles, and storylines that no one else can, but this was all too tragic and real.

Heels in life can beat you down to the point where you just don't care anymore about your performance on the job or your job overall. They can create this miserable environment where being loyal and hard working means nothing. It is whoever is kissing their ass. There's no right way to deal with it. If you fight, you could get fired. If you just take it, you stay unemployed. Admittedly, I've kept my mouth shut to keep a job. I may not be proud of it, but in the end, you have to decide what is more important.

People stabbing others in the back with one hand while shaking the other can happen in any business. I've been in the wrestling business 40 years, so I don't know what happens in other businesses. Hell, I don't even know what a gallon of milk costs. And I'm the one giving advice on the pages of this book.

I always knew that I could get stabbed in the back if I was in the main event because the person doing the stabbing wanted to be in my position. I can honestly say that I never stabbed anybody in the back. I really didn't. I just didn't mess with that part of life and had better things to do. I learned a long time ago that if you do stab someone in the back, you may have to get in the ring with them some day. "Accidents" can happen and they can happen right between the eyes.

I think anyone has the ability to stab somebody in the back. Everyone at some point has larceny in them. It's a matter of what you let the other person do to you. Do you let them beat you down? No. You remember the old saying of keeping your friends close and your enemies closer? I make friends with my enemies. At least I know where they are. If I don't talk to my enemy, then I don't know what he's up to.

That's how I get through difficult situations and people—just watching, listening, and communicating. I've found that it makes life easier if you maintain an awareness of what's going on around you. It seemed to me that everyone was jealous of others in the wrestling business and fewer would bother to help another person. During my wrestling career, I could always tell when someone was jealous of another. One guy would come into a dressing room with a new suit and tie or a new wrestling jacket that he was going to wear to the ring. Three guys would walk up and say, "Hey, nice-looking outfit you got." Another guy would walk up and ask, "How are you doing?" and say nothing about it. You know they saw it, but they didn't bother with a compliment. They just didn't want to put you over.

Heels are insecure. If someone is looking or doing better than they are, they see more what they don't have than what the other person has. Compliments are rare. They just stew about stupid things. Anger builds up and they develop an extremely thin skin when it comes to their short-comings and their enemies.

Heels will hold grudges forever. They will refuse to talk to someone over stupid misunderstandings, drawing a line in the sand or burning a bridge. No one knows why there is heat between Jesse Ventura and Hulk Hogan. I'm sure Hogan has his version of the story. Jesse has his version of the story. And they'll probably never sit down, shake hands, and talk. That is a true shame, because they both are going through their lives and missing out on another human being and what they have to offer. They are both interesting people who have lived amazing and unbelievable lives. They may be funny and intelligent. We all can learn from others, both good and bad. And for Hogan and Ventura to be so-called enemies and not speak to each other means that they're missing out on some things that the other knows. Those enemies are anything but close.

You can learn something every day if you listen to someone, whether you like to hear it or not. Don't just talk. Listening will get you every-thing. You have to listen to people, especially heels, to learn something or even if they make mistakes. You can capitalize on that, embarrass that heel for it, or even help out a friend who's dealing with his own heel. Talking won't get you anything but tired. Sometimes, talking will just get you in trouble. That's why there are attorneys out there who make $200 an hour.

Talk about heels. That's what I hate about the courts. If I went to a court over beating up some guy because a friend said that he said some-thing bad about me, that information would be inadmissible because it's hearsay. Well, what is an attorney doing then? He or she commits hearsay and is well paid for it. That attorney wasn't there when the alleged crime was committed, but he's in court swearing your innocence and doesn't really know you. The lawyer is in court because he wants to see the dead presidents, not because he's a friend.

One of my most famous lines is, "A friend in need is a pest." I've never had the chance to explain what I mean by that. A true friend would never be a pest necessarily. Sometimes a "friend" will ask someone to pick him up at the airport, loan them money, or perform any other type of favor.

Honestly, a "friend" in that kind of "need" is a pest.

Relatives are not much better. I've never had a problem, because I have great relatives. Some pest-like relatives keep asking and asking and asking for money, jobs, or help. They should pull themselves up by their own bootstraps sometimes, but they won't and will exploit the fact that you're related to the miserable bums. People I've known have loaned money to their relatives and did other favors, but never got paid back because their relative/pest claimed that they didn't have it. Actually, they take advantage of someone related to them.

A neighbor in need can be a pest, too. They will come over and drink all your beer, but never invite you over for beer. They'll invite themselves over for your barbeque, but never have you over for dinner. They'll invite you to their daughter's graduation and wedding, but all they want is a gift. But they won't show up for any event of yours that forces them to buy a gift.

That's what I mean by "a friend in need is a pest." They're not really friends after all. They're just people in need and willing to take advantage of others. That's a pest.

It's so easy to be a friend. It's not about money or jobs. A friend should be there for another friend. You don't have to tell a person all the time that you're a friend. You just are and they should know it. If they don't know it, that's their problem. If they take advantage of it, they're a pest.

As much as you want to beat up those heels in your life, you could end up with your ass in jail or you could really hurt someone. That's why I chose to play pranks on them. There are so many things you can do to someone to send a message to them but not really hurt them. Now I've dealt with a fair share of heels and pests who were anything but friends. In fact, they were people I dealt with every day in life.

In school, there was a kid in my class named David. He would beat me up all the time for no reason. He was a punk and I didn't like him. I realized that while I couldn't take the guy in a fight, I did know how to get him. So I took my pencil box and put it in his desk. When class started, the teacher would ask me to do something. I'd say, "I can't find my pencil box."

She would say, "Well, let's look and find it." She would look around the class and eventually found it in David's desk. That little heel would get in trouble. He didn't realize that it's not nice to mess with a weasel, especially a young one.

Another kid from my neighborhood would always park his bike by our house, chain it to the pole, and walk to the beach that was a block away. Every time he showed up, he would always make fun of my grandma because she was heavy. I didn't like the guy. In fact, I grew to hate him the more he made fun of my grandmother. It was time to deal with this heel, so I got some tin snips and cut all his spokes in half on both wheels.

When he got back from the beach, he would unlock his bike and ride away—or try to anyway. He didn't get too far without spokes.

Within a half hour, he was beating on my door. For some reason, he was positive I did it.

Across the street, there was a neighbor who didn't like me for any reason whatsoever. I honestly never did anything to deserve his hatred. I found out later that he thought I was breaking in the windows of his house. I didn't do it. I was surprised anyone could even understand this hillbilly since he pronounced the word windows "winders."

After his "winders" got broken again, he found me, grabbed me by the nape of the neck, and threw me on the ground. He really hurt me. I was only 14, and he was a much bigger guy. After it happened, I calmly plotted a way to get back to him. At first, I would order the whole family 10 pizzas from 10 different restaurants and have them delivered. Or I would call cabs for them around 9 p.m.

For me, that wasn't enough for "Winders." I got my hands on some Quaker Oats and put it in the radiator of his car. When his radiator heated up, the oats would spill over and it looked like his car was throwing up. I would also put limburger cheese on his engine block, so when he started his car, it would heat up to very aromatic levels.

The funny thing was "Winders" never bothered me after that, and I always wondered if he knew it was me to begin with. After he threw me down and I pulled all these pranks, I decided to make friends with him. Again, I was keeping my enemies closer. I'd always give him a smile and a wave because I wanted him to think that I would be the last person to do anything to him.

Remember, you get more laughs with sugar than you do with flies…or something like that.

I mentioned earlier about making friends with cops. I also tried to be friendly with the security guards as well. They had a tough and thankless job, too. But there was this one guy who never remembered me. Every time I tried to get into the building, he would ask me for identification or who I was with.

"Sir," I said. "I have been coming here for two years. I have bleached blonde hair and I'm wrestling tonight. You think I just did this to my hair to sneak into this place? You see me here every month. I see you and remember who you are. You know who I am."

He said, "Well, it's my job."

"Fine," I said.

When I walked in to the building, I saw this big-time card machine where we dressed in the back. I wanted to get back at the guy and had nothing to do, so I clocked everyone out, including him. I think he "punched out" at noon.

Sometimes having fun with heels doesn't work. At that point, you just need to walk away from people. There are a lot of individuals you can't have fun with, no matter how annoying they are or you are or how hard they make your life. There are a lot of people who will do that and you just have to turn your back and ignore them. It works. People hate it more than anything when you ignore them. They don't mind getting in an argument with you, but they don't like being ignored. In fact, they hate it.

Just give your enemies enough rope to hang themselves, but never let them defeat you. I told myself that throughout my life.

I've seen perfectly decent guys completely change for the worst because of success or someone else's influence. Hell, I've seen it in wrestling all the time. The Ultimate Warrior—who is a real jerk—would come into the dressing room and introduce himself to everyone when he first started. He seemed polite and respectful, but he was kissing up and manipulating people. When he became a main eventer and won the WWF title, sure enough, he stopped doing that.

He would say, "I don't need to shake anyone's hand."

I told him, "Do you think we ever wanted to shake your hand? We're just being polite."

None of us really liked him in the first place.

He wasn't much better in the ring, simply because he wasn't raised or probably even trained to be a wrestler. He wasn't in the business because he loved wrestling. He was just another guy who lifted weights and saw wrestling as an easy way to make some quick money. I'll give him credit. He had a great body, the face paint looked good, and his hair was nice and long. But once you got past the superficial stuff, everything stopped with him. All flash and no substance. Once that bell rang, it was over, and he was exposed for what he was. He never came across as an athletic kind of guy even though he had an athletic body. He was clumsy all the time, and I mean *all* the time.

On top of that, he wouldn't listen. I would say, "Don't clothesline me because I have a bad neck. When I jump onto the apron, come up to me from behind and run me into the post."

Naturally, he would run at me from behind and clothesline me. After the match, I would confront him in the dressing room, "Hey," I would yell. "Why the hell did you do that when I told you not to? I wasn't prepared for the bump."

He said, "Because I never know where I'm going to be."

Doing "Weasel Suit" matches with Greg Gagne in the AWA was easier than with the Warrior in the WWF because he didn't know how to work. That made it harder to work an angle with him, let alone a match.

Andre the Giant took care of him for me, though. During their match, Warrior would usually clothesline him into the ropes and Andre would make it look like he was all tied up in them. Warrior would then run at him at 200 miles per hour and nail him hard. Andre would let it go for the first two nights, but on the third night when Warrior was coming at him, Andre put up his hand and yelled "No" in this big, booming voice. That rattled Warrior's brain. The next night Warrior moved very slow.

Andre looked at me from the ring and said, "He's learning."

Warrior also learned that if Andre didn't want you to have a good match, you were completely screwed. Still, I don't think Warrior gained any respect for Andre or learned how to respect others in the wrestling business. Where is he now? Isn't he some wannabe Rush Limbaugh? And how is that wrestling school of his doing?

A lot of guys will come into a locker room and not only refuse to shake hands, they would start blabbering, "When I did this," and "When I did that," just putting themselves over. That's fine, but you can see how money and different stages of life affect people.

You learn how to survive and do the best you can with what you have. The best I could do is to make friends with people. I could make them laugh and make them talk to me. Instead of going out of my way to make enemies with people, I tried first to make friends with them. Sometimes that didn't work, but I always had people around and knew what they were doing. Somehow, we built trust, but not always friendship. No matter what, I'm not going to betray anybody's trust.

But if you start messing around with me, I may have to put my pencil box in your desk.

CHAPTER 15

Don't Be a Jobber

In the '70s, I was wrestling for a guy named the Bear Man, whose bear eventually ate his wife. I mention that not because it's funny, but because it's ironic. He was a promoter up in Canada and he ran things very loose. He would pretty much let you do what you wanted to do. The Bear Man was a good payoff guy and a nice man. He only ran in Ontario during the summers because it was hard to get around there in the winters. Baron Von Raschke, Blackjack Mulligan and I would work in Indianapolis, Detroit, and throughout Ontario. We'd pick up a couple hundred bucks a night and the Bear Man would pay for our gas. It was a new territory for us and we got to see different places.

The Bear Man would often use Bull Johnson, a "jobber" who was about 60 years old. He just wanted to give Bull a payday. Bull would pull up in his truck about one minute before his match—which was always the opener—wearing his wrestling boots, jock strap, a top, and a towel. His opponent would be in the ring and Bull would get out of his truck and head straight for the ring. He worked about two minutes, got beat, and would go right back to his truck, which he had left running the whole time.

A jobber in wrestling is not real, because wrestling is not real. So, he's not really being beaten by anyone. He's playing a character, like I portrayed a manager and a wrestler. A jobber—also known as jabroni, extra, and enhancement talent—is playing the part of getting beat all the time. He represents someone who is lying down in the ring for his opponent and losing all the time.

"I don't need anyone to make a fool out of me."

Why does a jobber play that role? Probably because for him wrestling is just a part-time job—something to be done on weekends. A jobber doesn't devote his whole career to it. Then, there are a lot of guys who did devote their whole career to it, but never got past that "jobber" status. It wasn't because they didn't have the ability to raise any higher, but no one would give them a break. I do believe that you will stay on the level you're meant to be. Some people will succeed. Some won't. If you could become president, you could, but you never know. I'm sure the first time George W. Bush crapped his diapers he didn't think he was going to be president.

To be a jobber in wrestling means that you will not win or overcome. Wrestlers worry too much about starting or ending their career as the guy who gets beat on television all the time. I guarantee you that most people who watch wrestling never know, see, or remember who is getting beat. They're watching the guy going over the jobber.

Like heels and babyfaces, jobbers aren't exclusive to professional wrestling. They are everywhere. Sometimes they're satisfied with their role in life and don't aspire to be anything more. That's wrong. In real life, no one should settle for being a jobber. No one should perform like they're in an enhancement match.

Why should you take a bump and lay on your back when someone else benefits from it? You have one shot in life. Take it and don't abuse it. Don't hurt people. Don't lie, cheat, or steal. And don't settle for second best, looking up at the lights with someone over you. Just do what the army says, "Be all that you can be," and do it for yourself.

Don't assume anything or expect anything from anyone. Don't look at the glass as half empty, which is a jobber attitude. Don't look at the glass as half full. Just don't look at it. It won't do you any good. Just hope that the glass is always full. Scotch would be my preference.

I've found myself acting like a jobber. One night I was in Winnipeg Arena and I had to get myself to the other side of the building for a radio interview scheduled right before the show. At the time, I had so much heel heat, I couldn't walk through crowds of people because they would have killed me. I couldn't go around the building for that matter. The only way was to walk across this catwalk that was high in the air. For some reason, I chose to do that.

I got to the top of the catwalk, looked down, and said, "Oh shit. I've got to do this interview. I've got to do it." It wasn't out of any obligation that I had. I was told to do it and, instead of explaining my fears of hostile crowds and catwalks to the promoter, I decided risking my life was a much better idea. Don't forget, I was a lot younger then and a lot dumber too. I was wrestling in the main event, but I was about to crawl on my knees like a jobber. I made it across and did the interview. When it came time to go back to the building, I avoided that catwalk and looked at the guy walking with me and said, "Hope you can keep up," I ran through that crowd of people as fast as I could. I didn't care if I got in a fight or got stabbed and shot. I walked so fast that they hardly saw me and if they did, they were shocked in that they never expected to see me there in the first place.

I should have said no to that situation. You have to stand up for yourself and say no. The option of, "Do it or you're fired," if it's a dangerous situation, is not an option. I never heard that from a promoter, but I guess I was fortunate.

Promoters are demanding, and it's only getting worse. In my day, the only thing we wanted to do is to take a bigger backdrop or bodyslam, get more blood, or get the best punch. Now, it's about falling through tables and off ladders and into thumbtacks and landing on cement. I'll bet that I could go up to one of these hardcore wrestlers and say, "We have a new idea this week. We're going to rub the cheeks of your ass with kerosene and ignite you. If you can come up with a flatulence, go ahead and shoot fire across the building."

Sadly, there would be way too many guys who would say, "I'll do it. I'll do it." That's the mentality. It's a jobber mentality even if they're going over in the main event because they're putting themselves at risk without thinking things through and standing up for themselves.

Sometimes, you may not want to dress up for an important meeting, so you wear tennis shoes. That's wrong. Put on a nice outfit and show that there is flash with the substance. You can always change after the meeting. Your first impression is your most important, and you don't get a chance to redo it. And if it doesn't work and someone doesn't like what you do, at the very least you can claim that you gave it your best shot. You didn't fail. They failed for not recognizing it and accepting you. You only fail if you don't try or set yourself up to fail or do the "job." Always, always, always think of yourself as better than a jobber.

There were times when I had to do a radio interview when I was on the road. I would think at first, "Hell, it's a radio interview. I'll wear a sweatsuit and running shoes." But if I were to walk into that studio and look like anyone off the street, then I would be nothing special. How much time does it take you to put on a pair of slacks, a clean shirt, a nice pair of shoes, and a sport coat? Let them say, "Wow, this guy is a professional at what he does. He must make some money too." Sure, I'm doing radio, but maybe in 10 years, the guy who interviewed me may be in management in radio or even television. Maybe he will remember me, and a door will be open for a new career. He remembered me not as a slob or jobber that slunk into his studio dressed like a bum, but as a professional.

The best way to spot a jobber is to see someone who is exactly the opposite. Some people complain that the bumps Shane McMahon takes on a television show or a pay-per-view steal the show. Let me tell you something, every night a performer is in front of the audience, he should be stealing the show. And if you see someone else stealing the show, steal it back from him. Or just step aside. When you walk into the office, steal the show. Get the big sale. Get the promotion. Hell, nail the secretary if you want to.

Don't ever be mediocre. Don't live your life like you're wrestling an opening match that no one cares about. Be a Shane McMahon who falls off the TitanTron and gets everyone to talk about him. I guarantee you that from McMahon to Bob Hope to the Rolling Stones, they never went out there like they were an opening act. That goes for Bill Gates, Donald Trump, and George Steinbrenner, too. They all "performed" like they were the main attraction, not a nameless, forgettable jobber.

I think a great deal of Shane. Honestly, I think he is the greatest heel manager in this business and someone I would consider to be the "Next Bobby Heenan." Because he is a winner—not a jobber—and has money. Everyone knows it. He's arrogant and a good-looking guy. And he can really work. He can take bumps and do a great deal in that ring. Besides, the bumps he takes don't just put him over, they put others over. That's what wrestlers and even fans never understand. On top of all that, Shane's got natural heat. No one likes the guy who's rich and the boss's kid. His dad is Vince McMahon, who owns the WWE. Shane would be perfect with the silver spoon in his mouth.

But as much as I admire him, there is a large part of me that wonders why he would want to be involved in the actual wrestling end of the business with all the money he is worth. I wouldn't take those bumps. Even Vince does it, because he loves it. In the early '60s, Dr. Jerry Graham bleached Vince's hair and gave him a red, ruffled shirt. There was Vince, driving in a convertible and smoking cigars. But the McMahons just want to be out there. They want to contribute. They want to win.

Right before Summerslam in Atlantic City many years ago, Vince was rehearsing a dance routine with professional dancers. He was even singing. He worked as hard at it as he did running his company. I watched him all day long and he really did a good job because he was confident and knew he could do it. That man is a professional.

Never count Vince McMahon out. He is anything but a jobber. The minute you think he can't do something, he surprises everyone and pulls it off with amazing success. From Wrestlemania and beyond, Vince has been a huge success. Yes, there have been World Bodybuilding Federations and XFL's along the way, but I'm sure he's learned from those mistakes.

But in today's wrestling landscape, I think Vince needs another wrestling group to compete against. He needs to be in a fight. That's where he thrives. He loves to outsmart his competition and loved getting to and finally buying WCW, but that took away a competitor. Competition gets his juices going and brings out the best in him, as it should anyone. Keep in mind that it's hard for a wrestling promotion to compete unless you have national television similar to what WWE has. Right now, there are only two major groups, if you count NWA-TNA. TNA stands for Total Non-Stop Action, but I think I know where they're going with those initials.

Tonsils and Adenoids.

I'm not sucking up to Vince for a job, because I don't really care if I work anymore. I just admire what he has done. For me to knock Vince in this book or on the air would be like knocking myself. The "powers that be" at WCW always wanted me to do it. I worked for him for 10 years and if I rip on him, what would that make me?

A jobber.

Vince and cable television made wrestling what it is today. I only know one other promoter who could have done it and didn't have that '50s mentality, which is get as many people as you can for the least amount of money. Run in the armory instead of going into the big buildings. The big buildings bring big crowds with them. I guarantee you that if you put the Ice Capades in an Armory, they'd sound like crap. Put them in Madison Square Garden and they would really sound like something.

Most promoters were small-time thinkers and jobbers themselves, because they were robbed by the promoters who robbed them. When they became promoters, they got their money back that they lost. How did they get it back? By robbing the next group of wrestlers. Robbing may be a little strong, but I suspected that they were either robbing us or, at the very least, not being fair.

Vince didn't kill the territories back in the '80s. He changed the industry and moved it into modern times. The promoters who resisted did the job to Vince in the middle of that ring. One-two-three. Vince didn't hurt them. He did what he had to do to compete, be successful, be happy, and not be a jobber.

You have to do what you have to do in life that makes you happy without hurting someone. If you hurt someone, lie to someone, or cheat someone, it may never come back to you. They talk about karma and what goes around comes around. I don't believe that. I've seen a lot of people do a lot of bad things and they continue with life. I've also seen a lot of good people who have suffered constantly. I don't believe in all that.

The only thing I can believe in is myself. That keeps me from being a jobber more than anything. But belief is a hard thing in this life. It's difficult to believe in yourself or anything for that matter, because there are so many distractions that make you not believe, whether it's people or just situations. I don't necessarily mean belief in God, it could be the government, your wife, your girlfriend, or your job. There are a lot of things you believe in that don't make sense.

The Pope drives around with bulletproof glass around him so no one will shoot him. Where is he afraid to go? He's been selling this piece of "real estate" to us for our whole lives and how great it is. He also says that we'll either have wings on our backs and fly or we'll be friends with a guy with a red suit and a tail. It doesn't make sense.

I'm not even sure praying works, because I have been praying a long time. I'm not an atheist, but I don't belong to a denomination. My whole family is Catholic and my brother was a priest. I just find it hard to see people suffering and no one helping. You hear about people with nothing who pray and do absolutely nothing bad in their whole lives. I'm sure multimillionaires who have conned people out of their money stay rich, successful, and happy. We can control what we do, say, and believe. In the world we live in, people will put 60 pounds of dynamite up their ass and do it in the name of their god. And others will pray about it for a week. Things I don't understand I don't mess with that much.

I sure hope there's someone up there. My mother-in-law, Conchetta, was a beautiful woman who owned 800 forks. She didn't know 800 people. Some said "Denny's." Some said "Perkins." She also had 900 ketchup packets in her drawer. At her funeral, I approached her casket and said, "Sweetheart, I think there's a pretty good chance that we'll never see each other again, because I will probably not be in the same place you are. I'll tell your mom hello for you because you probably won't see her, either."

There are people who claim they can talk to the dead. Let's see if I can figure that one out. Here's a guy who was born just like you, pissed his pants until he was four just like you, and went to school and spilled his milk on his shirt just like you. Suddenly, he can talk to everyone taking a dirt nap. He may think he can, and he may very well be insane, but we don't know because we're not in his mind.

The most secretive thing in the world is a person's mind. There are things in my mind and in everyone's mind that no one will ever know. Yes, I'd like to be tied up to a duck with a skate key, but no one needs to know that. No one knows what goes on in anyone's mind. So, how can a psychic even say, "I know what you're thinking"? You never know what anybody is thinking.

But people need something to believe in because they're looking for something. They're hurt and lost or they are failing in life and looking up at the lights like that wrestling jobber. If someone can pat their head and rub their back and say, "Bertie is talking to you from Cloud Nine," that can make them feel better. But it's not real. They are being exploited and primed for that three-count. I believe they don't have enough strength in themselves. They are very weak. It's similar to the guys who ask if they had a good match.

These people need help. They need guidance and strength. They need to move up on life's wrestling card from jobber to mid-card or main event. And the only way that can happen is if people around them are direct with them—good or bad—and maybe even a little harsh. Tell them what they do well and what they don't do well. Tell them what you do well and what you don't do well. They say that the truth will set you free. I say that the truth and only the truth will give someone else strength, whether they want to hear it or not.

There are good people and bad people, and I believe that everyone has the capability to change based on the situation. I don't care who it is or what they say as far as what they would or wouldn't do. If I found a wallet with a hundred grand, I'd return it because that person might need it. Now, "The Brain" would fight me on that, but I'd do it. I guess he would be a jobber. Hell, he did a job for Kenny "Sodbuster" Jay. Returning something that doesn't belong to you is a natural thing to do, and what a great feeling it can give you. Simply put, you do it because you should do it. No reward. No big news story. Just do what you should do.

Always remember, don't take second place. Who was the first man on the moon? Neil Armstrong. Who was the second man? Very few know. Main event gets the money, the first match doesn't. Top guys make the money. The bottom guys—or jobbers—don't. The one way to make sure that you're not a jobber is to get an education. Knowledge is power and knowledge is gold, figuratively and literally. If I know more than the next guy, I've got a leg up on him. That's the way life is. You've got to be a winner in life. People like winners and want to be around them. Put yourself in that position. Underdogs make for a good story, but the reason that they're in an underdog position is because they weren't as successful as the winners. If you call someone to shampoo your rug, will you call a company that may go out of business tomorrow or someone with a multimillion dollar company known as the best?

People know when you're a jobber or a loser. You act like it and look like it. Those guys have to have hot coffee thrown in their face. You have to wake up to the fact that you're a human being with a brain that can benefit others. You may not have a high IQ, and maybe you don't need one. But there is something you can do other than to accept that you are going to be a loser. If you want to accept it, then you are the definition of a jobber.

Losers and jobbers bring you down. Winners bring you up. If you hang around with successful people like Vince McMahon and Donald Trump, you'll start dressing like them and thinking like them. If you hang out with Bill the Bum in some alley, drinking a bottle of Mad Dog 20:20, all you are going to do the next day is figure how you're going to get more money for more Mad Dog. That's just the way life is, and those are the choices you have. Drink in the alley with Bill the Bum or ride in the big car with Trump and McMahon. Be a winner or loser. Be a main eventer or a jobber. It's your choice. It always has been and always will be.

I am proud to say that I never gave up my whole life, except two years ago. It all started when I found out that WCW was not going to renew my contract. Some people knew it and betrayed me by not saying anything to me. It wouldn't have made a difference, but I should have been told by the people I thought I could rely on. I realized that my career as an athlete in the ring was over long ago, so my plan was to stay in the business on the broadcasting end until I was 60, 70, or until I couldn't do it anymore or didn't want to do it. Gordon Solie did it for a long time. John Madden continues to announce for the NFL.

I had called WWE, and they didn't return my calls. I began to think to myself, "What have I done wrong? I was nice to people there and never knocked their product or Vince." It was also around that time that my speech started to get worse. The food I was eating was tasting differently, and I had no idea what was wrong with me. On top of that, my daughter was just about to get married, and there I was without a job.

As we got closer to the wedding, I decided to go to the doctor and I was diagnosed with throat cancer. My head was spinning. My wife had just had cancer a couple of years earlier, but we had insurance at the time. Now, I had to worry about insurance running out, let alone what the outcome of this disease would be. On top of that, my wife was diagnosed a second time in April of 2002. I had surgery on my throat in March of that year, only to have to go back in December of 2002.

I think after that, it really hit me. It was in January or February of 2003 that a cyst—just a fatty tissue or calcium deposit—on my hip that I always had from taking bumps grew to the size of my fist and became black after my chemotherapy and radiation treatments. The doctors told me that I had to have it removed. It forced me to miss the funeral of Curt Hennig—a close friend whom I loved dearly—because I couldn't sit on an airplane for a long amount of time due to all the stitches. It was so hard to take, on top of all the cancer surgeries, getting my lymph nodes taken out, and operations on my neck, knee, arm, and collarbone.

My daughter just got married and just got a new job. She was trying to make ends meet. My wife got sick again. I didn't know if she could keep working and, if that wasn't horrible enough, I was still facing my insurance running out. There didn't seem to be a wrestling organization out there anymore for me, and the main one out there wouldn't return my calls. And my speech was getting worse. That was very hard to deal with. I prided myself on my announcing and ability to cut an interview. It was my livelihood and the very idea of having to refer to it in the past tense cut me more than anything.

I wanted to give up. One day, I told myself while I sat at home, "You know what? There's nothing out there to do. And if there was, there's nothing I can do about it. Most of my friends don't live around me. My family can't do anything about this. I have no visible means of support. I know what to do.

"I'm just going to sit in this room and wait here to die."

After I went through that proclamation and laundry list, I slept as much as I could. Being unconscious took away the pain and to me, it made life go faster so I could get it over with. That day, I told my wife when she came home of what I had decided. I had a feeding tube in me for Christ's sake. I told her not to feel sorry for me because I was feeling sorry for myself. I told Cindi over and over again, "I'm not going to get better. I'm not going to get better.

"I don't care if I die," I continued. "My whole life I tried to support my mother, grandmother, aunt, you, and Jessica. I've tried to help out everybody and be there for everybody. And now I'm struck down with this. Why? Why me? It's like prison. I get three squares a day."

She kept telling me that I was doing fine, but that didn't work.

My friends—the Benjamins, the Goodwyns, and the Farmers—called. They would call me periodically. I broke down every time I was on the phone, "I can't eat. I have no job. I have no life. My daughter has moved out. My wife has to work so we can get insurance and she's sick. I don't know how much longer I'll have her. There's no reason for going on." They kept telling me there was, but that's the natural thing to do.

It didn't work either. Any friend would try to be reassuring, but that's what friends are for. Besides, they didn't know what was going through my mind and my body.

Then, my daughter came over. She knew what was going on because Cindi told her. "How are you feeling dad?" she asked.

I was direct and told her straight out, "I'm sick. I'm not going to get better."

She said, "No, you're not. You're probably going to die tomorrow."

"What?" I said. I was shocked that she would say that.

"That's the way you want to feel, feel that way. I don't want to hear it. I have my life ahead of me, and you're still going to be in my life and so is mom. So, every time you tell me how sick and bad you feel, tough shit. You're just going to get better."

Those words hit me and hit me hard. This girl whom I tried to give advice to and be an example for on how to live her life had just taught me a valuable lesson. She said out loud what I was thinking, and it didn't sound right at all. She threw it all in my face. I was talking and acting like the world's biggest jobber.

"You know, you're damn right. Nobody wants to hear this, do they?" I asked her.

"No, there's nothing that anyone can do for you that you can't do for yourself," she said.

"Thank you honey," I said. It was the most sincere thank you that I ever gave anyone. She may have very well saved my life by talking to me with such passion and anger.

And it was on that day that I wrote her out of the will.

In all seriousness, I did say "the hell with it." She was the one who turned me around. She didn't want to hear it. She gave me a kick in the ass and that's what people need. I needed to look at myself and the situation. She was right. Then again, being Bobby Heenan's daughter, she did the natural thing after she lectured me. She set me on the road straight, took my cancer survival kit, and sold it on Ebay.

From that point on, I tried to be up about things. What did I have to be upset about? No wrestling office would hire me. So what? Maybe I don't want to work for any wrestling office. I want to write a book, talk to people, and entertain. I've got a great writer doing the writing for me, and I look forward to this book being as good or better than the last one. That means buy it, you deadbeats.

I got over it. Ironically, it was Jessica who pulled me out of the other low point in my life when I lost my mother. At the age of four months, she helped me to go on. Looking forward to her future helped me deal with the past. Years later, my family did it again. You have to turn back to your family sometimes, not to mention your friends. Don't call a 900 number psychic and don't go to the church for advice. Priests can't get married. How can they tell you how to deal with family? It's like asking Bobby the Brain to hold your wallet.

Family comes through every time. At least they better. Someone needs to pull your shoulder off the mat so you don't lose life's wrestling matches.

CHAPTER 16

Grappling with What Scares You and Standing Up for Yourself

I was terrified of the AWA plane and after all that had happened, I had had enough. I wasn't willing to face that fear anymore, but I was going to take a stand. I told Verne that I could not fly in a low-flying plane anymore.

When you are looking to succeed, there will be times when you have to put your foot down, no matter what the consequences. Success in your profession is a wonderful thing, but if you took shortcuts or did things you were ashamed of, where is the reward? I never liked to make trouble and usually did what I was told when it came to my job. The payoff at the end of the night motivated me. But there were times when I had to draw the line.

When I was with the WWF around 1990, Vince McMahon came up with this idea to have me handcuffed to the security rail that kept the people back in the arena. At that time, I was involved in a program with the Big Bossman where I was constantly insulting his mother. Vince's idea was for Bossman to rip my clothes off me and leave me standing there handcuffed in my underwear. He wanted me to have hearts on my underwear, almost like women's panties. At first I said, "Fine."

"A pat on the back is only 12 inches from a kick in the rear."

When you're used to agreeing with the plans all the time, sometimes you don't think things through. Being agreeable makes you a nice guy, but sometimes, nice guys can get stepped on and hard.

The next day we were in Providence, Rhode Island. I started to think about the angle that Vince proposed. The more I thought about it, the more I didn't like it. There were two reasons. First, it doesn't fit with the Bobby Heenan character, because no one never gets heat, and it's never entertaining to be embarrassed. People want to see his ass kicked, but why watch him be uncomfortable? Second, my daughter was enrolled in a Catholic school at the time. What were her friends going to say about her dad wearing heart underwear? Would it embarrass her?

I made a very tough decision and did something I thought I would never, ever do, especially to Vince McMahon. I invited him into the dressing room. We sat down and I gave him my final answer on the angle, "Vince, I just can't do it."

He sat there for the longest time, before finally breaking the silence.

"You can't do it?" he asked.

"No."

The silence was deafening, so I decided to break it by offering an alternative, "Why don't you just handcuff me to the ring and just leave me there for the whole hour? When someone would come to the ring, I'll say, 'Will you go get Rick Rude or one of the members of the Bobby Heenan Family?' In the meantime, all the babyfaces can come out and play with me or pretend to hit me. It would work out great."

Vince sat there and listened to me telling him why I don't want to do the hearts on the underwear thing and strip down. Basically, he was listening to someone giving him a long and elaborate "no."

He said, "You won't do it?"

"Vince, I can't do it."

"Bobby," he tried to explain. "It's a work."

"I know that, Vince," I said. "But if it's a work, then you can change it. I can't do it. It would be too hard on my kid."

"You can't do it," he said again.

"No," I said.

Without saying another word, he stood up and walked out and slammed the door so hard that the building shook.

I wasn't doing it no matter what. Vince was very upset with me that I told him no. I didn't tell him no because I disrespected him or anything. I just couldn't do something that I'm not comfortable with and then go out and make it look good. I never wrestled as a cowboy or a German because that's not me. I don't look good in Western clothes and I can't speak with a German accent.

My character of Bobby the Brain is a loudmouthed, brash manager. I'm not a prissy little guy like some managers are. And I not only play a manager, but a wrestler too. I felt my reputation was at stake and I had never done anything like that before throughout my career. I think whoever thought of the idea wanted to make "Bobby the Brain" look gay or make people suspicious while they stared at the hearts on the women's underwear I would be wearing. That didn't sit well with me. I didn't know how to act with all the people staring at me and laughing. I don't think I could have pulled it off.

It wouldn't have worked, and I didn't want to do it. I'm sure bigger people than me said no to Vince McMahon and lived to tell about it.

In the end, I think he accepted it because I was doing so many things and he didn't want to lose me. I was managing almost every top heel there. I was doing Wrestling Challenge, Prime Time, and the pay-per-views. I was directing talent and producing the interviews. Plus, I was wrestling and managing.

In the end, the angle I suggested is what we did, and it told a great story throughout the whole hour that incorporated a bunch of different stories where I was begging the babyfaces to help me. I would offer them 50 bucks or kiss up and compliment them on the trunks they were wearing. Rick Rude finally came out, but he didn't have a key to help me. He just screamed at McMahon to go get it.

I guess if Vince had given me an ultimatum, I would have left. It would immediately tell me right off the bat that there was no respect or regard for me and for what I do. I had enough regard for him to be up front and say I couldn't do it. I offered another idea and gave him an entire day to change things, so we could do business and work something out. I gave him what I thought was a better idea and something I was comfortable doing. It was much more entertaining.

Some people just don't like to be told no. Vince was open enough to accept my alternative, but I know he didn't like it when that building shook.

When Vince slammed that door, I thought, "I'm done." I walked up to Jack Tunney afterwards and practically said goodbye to him. Tunney said, "No, don't worry about it." I told Lanza what I had done. He wasn't sure what to think. For the whole day, I just sat up in the stands so Vince couldn't find me. I finally walked downstairs about 3:00 to start producing the interviews. Nothing was ever said about it after that.

Maybe he never planned to fire me, but he sure slammed the door like I wasn't coming back.

Standing up for yourself is important, even if what you're doing is unpopular. You have to stand by what you believe in. Even if the consequences are not what you want, at least you can say that you stuck by your guns. It can be scary, but you have to face your fears to fight for what you believe in.

As scary as Vince could be when he was angry, nothing really scared me more than the old AWA plane. And it was another moment where I wasn't just going to accept things as they were presented to me.

Verne Gagne owned this twin engine Navajo Chief that held eight people, counting the pilot. I used to call it "Suicide One." We would be flown to places such as Omaha, Chicago, Milwaukee, Winnipeg, Ottawa, Peoria, Moline, Green Bay, and sometimes Denver. It wasn't pressurized, so you couldn't go over 10 feet.

One day, we all overheard Verne asking the pilot, "Can we take the plane to San Francisco?"

The pilot said, "We can't go over the mountains. We're not pressurized. You'll lose your oxygen. The only way I can do it is to fly way south through Phoenix."

Baron Von Raschke overheard the conversation and said, "Do you realize that by the time I get there, I'll have a head of hair?"

That plane was bad sometimes and a nightmare all the time. You just bounced around so much. One time, Raschke tightened up his body so much out of pure fear, he injured himself by pulling all the muscles in his back. It even smelled bad in that plane, probably from everyone sweating over fear. The best way I could describe the smell is something like bad lamb. Sometimes you found yourself kissing your own ass up there. God, it was so horrible. Sure, it would get you there, but on some nights, I swear I don't know how we made it.

One time, when we flew to Canada, we couldn't get off the plane because someone had to inspect the piece of shit. We had to sit in that plane and the pilots couldn't keep it running during the inspection. We sat there a half hour before we could go through customs. Maybe Canadians don't understand it, but normal people don't like to sit in the cold.

We also found out that the pilot Verne originally hired worked for another airline, and they had fired him because he couldn't handle himself in stressful situations. But Verne thought he was good enough to fly my ass to Green Bay.

We would ask this idiot how long the flight would be and he would always say, "An hour and 20 minutes. We're going to fly like a jackrabbit. Whooee! Holy cat's meow!"

This nut was flipping all over the place. He would fly us right through the goddamn thunderheads instead of avoiding them. The other pilot would at least leave an hour early so we could fly around them.

Meanwhile, we switched seats 12 times on that plane, but not deliberately. It was just so bumpy.

When we would land in Green Bay or Milwaukee in the wintertime, there wasn't always a hangar available, so "Suicide One" would have to sit outside. Everyone who was going to ride on the plane would leave the building and make their own stops for cheeseburgers, chips, or a case of beer so they all had what they wanted. If it happened to be a snowy night, we would have to all grab a broom and clear off the wings.

We would get into the plane and shut the door as it started to taxi out. Keep in mind that in the winter, it was usually zero degrees or colder. I was walking around in a snowmobile suit and moon boots like Frankenstein. When we would get to the end of the runway, the pilot would yell, "Now." We'd all jump out of the plane, take our arms and clean the snow off the wing again, this time while it was moving. The snow was still coming down hard. Then, we'd jump back in the plane, shut the door, and the pilot would take off.

One night we were taking off from the Minneapolis airport. I was on the plane with Pampero Firpo, Larry Hennig, Raschke, Nick Bonkwinkel, Don Jardine, and Angelo Mosca. We were told that the mechanics had just put a new fuel pump on the plane. What we didn't know is that the pilot never took the plane up by himself to test it out. We took off and the plane immediately started shaking. We heard him yell, "It's the fuel pump. Mayday! Mayday!"

We all thought that was it and we were going to buy it. "Suicide One" was about to take us out once and for all. Firpo and I are holding each other. I was looking out the window and could see how close we were to the local houses as they tried to return us to the airport. I could see a guy eating his TV dinner, watching the news with Walter Cronkite. It was a turkey, mashed potatoes, and stuffing. That's how close I was.

If the smell of the plane wasn't bad enough, Firpo was Armenian, and when an Armenian man's sweat glands kick in, it's like nothing you ever experienced before. I'll guarantee you that the back ass end of Bin Laden's robe that he has been sitting on for the past five years in a cave does not compare to the aroma of a terrified Armenian.

Now that I think about it, it may have been me. And it may not have been sweat.

While we landed safely that time, the plane itself was still frightening enough without some of the passengers acting up, including Mad Dog Vachon, who really lived up to his name on one flight. We were flying from Denver to Rapid City, South Dakota on our way to Minneapolis. The plane was supposed to leave at 4 p.m., but someone forgot to tell Mad Dog. He arrived at the airport, but the plane had already left. He had to go back and buy a ticket with his own money. He would have been reimbursed, but that didn't stop this dog from foaming at the mouth. Everyone else waited in Sioux Falls for a couple of hours for him to fly in, because we saved a place on the plane for him.

He finally showed up.

"Didn't anybody tell you when we were leaving?" somebody asked him.

"No one told me," he growled.

To say he was mad is an understatement. On top of that, he had a few beers before he even got on the plane to get to Sioux Falls. He ended up sitting in the back with Adrian Adonis, who was a great ribber. One of the best. He must have got Dog all stirred up, teasing him on how he was left back in Denver. It obviously got to be too much for him.

Some of the wrestlers on the plane—Jesse Ventura, Greg Gagne, Adrian Adonis, Nick Bockwinkel, and Lord Alfred Hayes—were playing cards. All of a sudden, the cards started flying around the plane. Mad Dog had opened both doors, one that was like a hatch and the other that was probably the stairs. It had a rope hanging off of it. In a rage, he began to throw all his wrestling gear out of the window and a nearby wastepaper basket. Imagine the farmer in Fort Dodge who woke up in the morning and found a pair of wrestling boots, a black pair of trunks, and a chain right next to his rutabaga and corn.

He probably pulled his kid playing the banjo off the porch and yelled at him, "This don't look right. There's Mad Dog on the back of some black underwear, roller skates without the wheels, and a chain. What have you been doing with the livestock, Elmer?"

Adrian didn't think things were so funny anymore. He actually thought that he was the next out of the plane for stirring up the shit. Mad Dog was standing there, hanging outside of the plane with the rope from the stairs around his neck, trying to pull the door up with his neck. Everybody was screaming and things were flying around.

The pilots were forced to land in Fort Dodge, Iowa. The pilot got off the plane and said, "Now guys, I have to know what happened. If the door opened by itself, we have a mechanical problem, and by FAA law, we can't take off. If one of you opened it up, just tell me. It's okay."

Then, he looked at Mad Dog. He was pretty sure that he did it. "If you opened it up, it's between you and the Minneapolis office when you get back. Not you and me."

That was probably the smartest thing he said.

"We can go home, but it absolutely cannot happen again," said the pilot. "Now, did you open the door?"

There was a long pause.

"Dog sorry," Mad Dog finally said.

The next day, Verne pulled Mad Dog in the office, "My son was on that plane. Half the roster was on that plane. You could have killed them all. Plus, you could have lost your own life."

"You will never be on the plane again," Verne commanded. "I don't care if you have to walk to the town. I don't care if you have to crawl to the town, but you'll never be on that plane again."

"I understand," Mad Dog said as he walked out of Verne's office. He then quickly turned around and said, "By the way, Verne, what time is the plane leaving?"

"What the hell did I just say?" Verne yelled.

"That's ok," Mad Dog interrupted him with a smile on his face. He was just trying to get to Verne one more time.

I love Mad Dog. He loves his name too, because of what it spells backwards.

He was eventually allowed back on the plane again because they wanted it full. But we kept him away from the goddamn door. Like we could stop him anyway. Even if we could keep him away from the door, he'd chew his way through the cockpit.

After all those incidents, Verne held a meeting where we discussed "Suicide One." Verne asked one guy, "What do you think of the plane?"

"Well, it's convenient and it saves money on motel rooms," the little kiss-ass said.

Another suck-up said, "I don't mind it."

Verne got to me and I was brutally honest, "I'm terrified. I'm terrified at the thought of going in there because of the thunderstorms in the Midwest."

He got to Firpo, who said, "Verne, it is a flying coffin. I've lost 20 pounds and I find myself drinking in the morning."

Verne's response was, "How big of a chicken are you?"

I responded with, "How many eggs do you need?"

If it wasn't bad enough flying on that deathtrap with wings, Verne actually charged us for the seat we occupied. He determined his "fare" based on what the airlines were charging at the time. After I refused to fly, Verne told me that he'd charge me double what I would have paid because there would be an empty seat now and he needed it full. You would think that the wrestlers would save money flying on a company plane. Not in the AWA. Not with Verne Gagne. Plus, he had insurance on every seat of that plane.

I never flew on it again. Billy Graham joined me in my "strike," but not the others. Ray Stevens loved that plane. The bumpier the better, yet he was afraid to go on a carnival ride. To this day, I still hate to fly. I'm still afraid of it in many ways. I know many pilots and the thought of them behind the wheel scares the shit out of me. I only do it because I have to.

Fear is a powerful thing. Standing up for yourself is frightening. Whether it is Vince McMahon or a wobbly "Suicide One" with some nut hanging out of it and dropping stuff. Put the two together and it can be a lethal and very interesting combination. Fear can stop you from standing up for yourself, but it can also force you to make a stand so you never have to be afraid again.

CHAPTER 17

Unleashing Your "Inner Brain"

After Slick, a manager with the WWF, left the company, he became a reverend and formed his own church. I even went to one of his services with Gorilla Monsoon and Vince McMahon, and it was really nice. Everyone got up and got loud. I was even yelling, "Hallelujah. Hallelujah, WWF!"

Vince told us that when they passed the offering plate around, put $100 in it to make sure Slick was taken care of. Monsoon put his hundred in and I started slapping my pockets.

"Monsoon," I said, "I left my wallet in my other pants."

He said, "Yeah, right," and put in a hundred for me. What I didn't know is that Slick was going to pass the offering plate again. When the plate came back to us, Monsoon put two hundred in again, looked at me and yelled, "I know. Your other pants."

I hate to admit it sometimes, but there is a lot of Bobby Heenan in Ray Heenan. I've been portraying this character for so long in this business that it can take over the Ray Heenan part of me. But I have to let him take over if I'm going to have any fun. I have to move a nameplate on a table and screw someone's seating arrangement up.

Unleashing your "Inner Brain" does not mean playing the "Bobby 'The Brain' Heenan" character. Sure, those types of antics may be lean-

"Sometimes this 'Brain' thing is a gimmick."

ing toward the heel side, but its just an opportunity to put a smile on your face or someone else's or to just blow off some steam. It's something we all do or should do from time to time. Unleashing your "Inner Brain" means to be mischievous, but in a fun way. It lightens your mood and hopefully the moods of others too, but not all the time, especially if they're on the receiving end of the "unleashing." Unleashing your "Inner Brain" also refers to entertaining people. That's what I've spent more than 40 years doing, and I often need my fix still to this day.

It requires a certain amount of creativity and the ability to think on your feet. And it's not always about doing necessarily the right thing. Those feet must be used sometimes to run out of the room if the "Inner Brain" in you has gone too far and may not have gotten the desired reaction. Some laugh. Some scowl. Some come after you.

Remember, unleashing your "Inner Brain," is not about being ethical. It's about being practical with a wicked grin on your face. Does it mean you act like a heel? Yes, but, like the song says, "Everybody plays the heel…sometimes," or something like that.

I have to unleash that "Inner Brain" and the heel side of me. I guess the best way to describe a true heel is to describe what it is like with a bunch of heels in the same room. Inevitably, if we are together after a match, we will all walk around limping. Bill Watts, who was a baby-face—or good guy—asked us one night why we were all limping. He didn't understand. As a babyface, he was a bump giver and heels were bump takers, Even Dick the Bruiser, an almost career babyface, would complain about the ring we worked in being so hard.

I asked him, "Who told you? You were never down on it. How would you know?"

I started playing the heel and unleashing that "Inner Brain" to take the bumps that life had to offer me at a very young age.

When I was a kid growing up in Chicago, there was a grocer located next to the apartment building called Abe's Delicatessen. He had these tanks that were filled with bottles of Coca-Cola. If you wanted a Coke, you had to put in a dime in the tank and then pull the bottle through this path to bring it up.

The wheels were turning in my head. I thought, "How can I get them out of there without paying?"

I didn't have any money, but I was thirsty enough to get my hands on a can opener and a straw. When no one was looking, I would open up the bottles while they were still in the tank and drink the Coke out of the straw.

My thirst was quenched, but this was an activity I grew out of. I was just a kid. My "Inner Brain" matured beyond stealing soda…or did it?

As I got older, I got more creative and elaborate with unleashing my "Inner Brain." When I worked at a department store, the delivery truck would show up at around 10:30 in the morning with all the merchandise. I usually took lunch from noon to 1:00, so you'll have to trust me that it was a major inconvenience. The guy in charge of the dock took lunch from 1:00 to 2:30, so it wasn't any better for him.

Keep in mind that to unload that truck took a couple of hours and I was lazy, even back then. So I would take the truck and park it by the freight elevator. At 11 a.m., I would go to lunch because I knew that the supervisor thought I would be loading the stockroom. He knew when my lunch hour was, so it worked out great. I would have a guy clock me out at noon after I left. Another buddy would clock me in at 1 before I even showed back up. I would do the same for them. During the times I would be paged, I would throw some water in my face and under my arms to make it look like I was sweaty from working so hard and found my supervisor.

My "Inner Brain" almost got me my first drink in a bar, even though I was underage. I was 18 and my friends dared me, saying that I could never do it. So I walked into the bar and sat down. The bartender said, "What can I get you?"

"How much is a Pabst Blue Ribbon?"

He said, "Get the hell out of here."

I learned that day if you buy and drink beer regularly, you should know how much it is. I should have stuck with Coke.

When I finally was old enough to be in bars, I would just love to scam people. The "Inner Brain" in me would take five pennies and put one on each corner of a napkin and one in the middle. Then, I would find some sap and say, "I'll tell you want. I'll bet you a drink that if you touch one of those pennies while I'm in the bathroom, I can come back and tell you which one you touched.

"No way," they'd always say.

So, I would leave and the sap at the bar would touch one of the pennies. What he didn't know was that I had a buddy or plant sitting at the bar too and he would take a drink of his drink and set it next to the penny that was touched. The only trouble with that is that if you screw people out of so many drinks or they figure things out, they would challenge you to a fight. I'm a ribber, not a fighter, and always knew when to leave.

The rock and roll bands would come into town, including "Dick Clark's Caravan of Stars" with the Dave Clark Five and the Hollies. I worked at the Coliseum and when I was on the job, I would wear a Beatles-like suit. Everyone would see me in the suit and think I was in the band. They would ask me to sign their programs. After I did that, I would always hear people say as I was walking away, "Who's Ray Heenan? And where's my pen?"

I had access to the dressing rooms. One night, I found a pair of drumsticks that were broke. The "Inner Brain" was unleashed. Right before the next show came to town, I bought 20 drumsticks. I'd walk out to the crowd and yell, "Hey, I've got Ringo's drumsticks" and sell them for 10 bucks.

Those poor people probably still have them. They may have them prominently displayed in their house or hanging on their wall, and with thumbtacks if it's my son-in-law. For all I know, they may be up for sale on some auction website. For those of you who bought them, they're not Ringo's drumsticks. They're Ray Heenan's drumsticks. If you bought this book and are reading this now for the first time, I'm sorry. If you mooched the book, you know what you can do with those drumsticks or you can feel free to put in a bid on Ebay.

When I finally became involved in professional wrestling, I portrayed the heel the whole time. I became the man everyone hated to hate from birth. I started in the industry in 1965, and just like every other actor looking for a break, I wanted to play a bad guy. To be a heel was just good, dirty fun. What I soon realized is that I had been heeling for several years before even seeing a wrestling ring.

During my early years in the business, I was always under the impression that I had to be a heel all the time, both inside and outside the ring. Promoters would tell me that I didn't want people thinking I was a good person, so it was drilled into me and everyone else. There are people in life who believe that without a promoter convincing them. They live the heel gimmick. That or something happened in their life or they've dealt with their own heels that they decided to become one 24 hours a day.

Sometimes, it was easy for me to turn that character on and off. But many times, I learned that even if I tried to be nice to someone, it didn't matter. They considered me a heel. That was difficult for me to overcome, and I'm sure it's hard for others to overcome as well. It brought out my "Inner Brain."

The perception that you're a bad person, even though you didn't do anything to deserve it is a challenge. People jump to conclusions as to the type of person you are based on what you do for a living or who you hang around with. They take one look at you and pass judgment, saying that they're a great judge of character. Or they're just plain ignorant.

I have also encountered my fair share of heels throughout my life as I mentioned earlier in the book. There are many different types of real-life heels that I've encountered in my life and times when I've had to play the heel away from the wrestling ring to my advantage. In a way, that's how "Bobby the Brain" would do it. But, unlike the character I played, I had to figure out exactly when the "Inner Brain" in me would and would not work.

I've often had to go to extremes to prove to people who didn't know me that I wasn't the person they saw in the wrestling ring. Just as a heel is a role you have to play from time to time, you have to show that it's not who you are all the time.

I worked in a territory where we had a ring announcer named Sam Menecker. He had a mother-in-law who had traveled from Hungary to live with him and she was a wrestling fan all the way. She used to watch me on television and go to the matches. This lady really grew to hate me. I would go over to Sam's house, and she would let me have it, thinking I was the character I played on television. No matter how hard I tried, there was no convincing this woman that I was Ray Heenan, not "Bobby the Brain."

I knew that I had to prove to her that what she saw on television was different from the person I really was. Explaining didn't work because she just wouldn't listen. So, I tried something extremely drastic and introduced her to my "Inner Brain."

Or my good-guy "twin brother."

When I visited the house, Sam and I would convince her that I was not Bobby Heenan, but Ray Heenan, essentially his babyface twin brother. The old broad actually bought it. She would even tell me how terrible my "evil twin" Bobby was and how much she hated him. She actually felt sorry for me for having such a miserable "brother." She even baked for me and fed me every time I would come by, but only if I identified myself as "Ray."

Speaking of twins, I dated a Siamese twin once, but she broke up with me when she found out I was dating her sister. She was sweet, though. She would go to England every six months so her sister could drive.

Even though Sam's mother never found out the truth, I was at least able to show her that there was another side to my personality. In a strange way, I guess lying to her like that made me a heel. Sure, I loved to play the bad guy in wrestling and in real life from time to time with fans who would want an autograph or shake my hand, but that's not who I was. While playing the heel can be important in certain situations, you can't do it all the time. That just makes you a jerk and no "Inner Brain" can help you.

I'm not saying I was never a jerk. I would often drive my Ford Falcon around downtown Indianapolis. There was this round street called Monument Circle where you were not allowed to park. While driving the circle, I saw a car from one of the local news stations with a big piece of cardboard on the windshield that said "WFBM Channel 6" news. The "Inner Brain" in me decided to take it for myself and that allowed me to park wherever I wanted to. The police would always assume that I was part of a film crew and I never got a parking ticket. I had a back-up plan too. If I didn't have the sign nearby, I would leave my hood open to make them think I was having car trouble.

I eventually replaced my Ford Falcon with a 1968 white Chevy Ford Nova with a stick shift. It was my first new car. During my last road trip with the Falcon, I was driving back from Fort Wayne with Bruiser, Wilbur Snyder, and Crusher. Crusher was sitting behind me while I was driving. He thought it would be funny to keep putting a paper bag over my head so I couldn't see the road. He kept doing it every 20 miles or so. Not satisfied with the bag, he reached back and pulled on my seat to shake me up a little. The only things shook up were the hinges, which broke from the force.

As I disappeared into the back seat onto Crusher's lap, the car veered off the road and into some mud, and we couldn't get it out. Crusher—now trying to be a help instead of being a pain in the ass—found a huge tree branch, jammed it under the front bumper, and tried to lift the car up with it, almost tearing my bumper off. He eventually got behind the wheel of the car, put it in reverse, and freed the car but barely missed two trees that he drove between.

I had to turn in this car to trade it in for my new one the very next day. Instead of admitting what had happened and losing value on the car, the "Inner Brain" in me put Coke cases in the back seat, so the seat would stay up and I could drive it to the dealership. I waved at the salesperson and he waved at me. When he wasn't looking, I took the Coke cases out of the car and put them in the trunk. I balanced the seat in an upright position, walked inside, signed all the papers, and shook on it. I got my new car and it was great. It smelled new and everything. As I was driving away quickly, I saw the salesman get in the car and shut the door.

Then he disappeared into the back seat.

Not only have I played the heel—or jerk in those instances—to my advantage, I've also found it fun to blow off steam and have fun unleashing my "Inner Brain." It never got me far with people, but I needed to kill time waiting for airplanes, rental cars, and hotel rooms. Sometimes, I got a little bored, stir crazy, and a little mischievous at times. It's just my nature.

Airports and airplanes were fun places to introduce everyone to my "Inner Brain." That is, if I wanted to get something for free. Whenever they had the booze cart on the airplanes, there was always a temptation to steal a few bottles while the flight attendant was pouring my drink and not paying attention to the cart. So, I would tell the flight attendant that I saw someone from the front of the airplane stealing bottles. She would be so appreciative; I would get a free drink out of it. No one ever got in trouble because I never specified who that thief was. One more bit of advice: Telling the flight attendant that you're there with your wife on your honeymoon always got you a free bottle of champagne.

Baron Leone, a wrestler from way back, used to use his "Inner Brain" and work up crowds too, just for fun. He was a heel in the ring, but he loved to play the agitator outside the ring. He would stand in hotel lobbies and, out of nowhere, start speaking about various issues. He would talk about things like how our government didn't take care of old people. Eventually, a crowd would gather around him and listen. They started nodding in agreement and even cheered Leone on, even though most of them had no idea who he was. Then, when he had the crowd in the palm of his hands, he would turn around and say things like, "But why should we help old people? They're just a burden on society. They're just going to die anyway. Besides, all they need is a glass of water to put their teeth in." Suddenly, his "Inner Brain" manipulated that crowd and turned them against him. It was a great lesson in psychology and sociology.

Mr. Fuji was one hell of a ribber, but his "Inner Brain" was a little more cruel. He was the kind of guy who would get back at you, but very, very slowly. It was like a Chinese water torture with Fuji. When we would work in a high school gym, Fuji would find a whole bunch of open padlocks from the lockers. He would put them through the belt loops of someone's pants or the button holes of their suit jackets. How are you going to get a padlock off your suit in Omaha at midnight? Plus, the damn thing added 10 more pounds to your pants.

I was doing *Hulk Hogan's Rock and Wrestling* cartoon show out in Los Angeles with Fuji, Freddie Blassie, and Gene Okerlund. For one of the live vignettes that they aired between the cartoons, Blassie had to get in an argument with a real old woman who would turn out to be his mom.

During a break, this poor old woman they cast to play Freddie's "mom" (and she had to be old to play the mother of Freddie Blassie, God rest his soul) stood up and asked where the bathroom was. She was pointed toward a door off the sound stage. While the woman was in there, Fuji and his "Inner Brain" both pushed a nearby Coke machine in front of the door. I don't know how long the woman was in there. Fuji decided to get the hell out of Dodge as this poor old woman was beating on the door. But no one could hear her. The only reason they found her was because she still had her wireless microphone on. The guys in the truck outside of the studio heard her screaming, but couldn't figure out where it was coming from.

This poor old woman finally got out of that bathroom, but it took a stagehand to finally move the Coke machine. The now sweaty old woman went straight home.

A heel like Fuji loved the reaction, good or bad. It feeds his "Inner Brain." When you unleash your "Inner Brain," you may get the reaction you want and you may not. Many people have asked me if it bothered me to hear boos from the crowd. Of course not. That was my job, and I loved every minute of it. You tell them to shut up, they jeer louder. You tell them to root for your wrestler, they do exactly the opposite and cheer on the other guy. While getting free drinks and riling up people to see your side of things doesn't help you in the long run, it sure was fun, and that's what life is about—having good, harmless fun and unleashing that "Inner Brain" on the unsuspecting public.

I really sicked my "Inner Brain" on people out of just pure fun when I was on a cruise with Nick Bockwinkel and our wives, but I also believed it would help the situation. The ship had stopped in a port, and we got off to do some sightseeing. After a while, I looked out to the ocean and saw a ship leaving. I nudged Nick and asked him, "Isn't that our boat?" We found out later that the anchor wasn't long enough and didn't hook to the bottom of the ocean. So, it had to leave and we were told to wait for about an hour. I thought that was ridiculous.

During that time, a bunch of people from the ship had gathered around where we were standing. When they all heard what had happened with the boat, they all seemed pretty calm and understanding about the whole thing. They weren't mad at all, and that was something I just couldn't understand. I thought they should be more assertive in complaining about what had happened and the inconvenience it caused.

So, my "Inner Brain" decided to stir them up a little bit. I started loudly complaining about the situation and the people started agreeing with me. To make matters better or worse, depending on whom you ask, I had bought a case of beer—or my "Inner Brain" did and used my money, the cheapskate—and shared it with them. Now, they were drunk and mad. When the ship came back, they were furious and they all demanded to see the captain.

Was the cruise ship wrong for leaving us stranded? Yes, and I wanted people to know it and understand it. I may have taken extreme steps to get there, but I got those people to stand up for themselves. I'm sure that cruise ship went out and bought a longer rope for their anchor after we got through with them. If no one was stranded again, I accomplished my goal.

Now you can't fight city hall or major cruise lines sometimes. Even some of these hotels are owned by huge corporations and have really lost the personal touch. One customer leaves them and promises that he'll never come back, the hotel will just get another one to replace him just from the influx of people coming in. So, when I'm frustrated with a hotel and its service, my "Inner Brain" likes to do little things. I would take the batteries out of the clicker. Whoever used it will never think it's the batteries, it would have to be the television. I'd also get behind the TV and turn the "bright" up. Whoever is watching could hear it and they could change the channels, but they couldn't see anything.

If I couldn't mess with the television, I would pull back the covers and sheets on a bed, down to the mattress pad. Then, I'd take a glass of water and pour it in the middle of the bed and make the bed again. When the maid came in, she would strip the bed down and make it again, but they never changed the mattress pad. Yes, it was juvenile and immature, but no harm done. And maybe it would wise some people up about staying in those hotels.

My attorney had as much of a sense of humor as I did and would always play pranks with me. He had an active "Inner Brain," but I would always get him back. We were staying in New York to testify before a grand jury and I had to pay for his hotel room, so I decided it was the perfect opportunity to set him up. I put him up at the Ramada at 49th and 8th in New York City. The hotel was right next to a fire station, so there was a lot of activity and noise. But that wasn't enough for my "Inner Brain." I told the lady at the front desk to give him a room by the elevator. I gave her some line about how he liked to be close to the elevator for safety purposes.

I had every right. I was paying, for crying out loud. The next morning, he said, "Thanks a lot."

"For what?"

"All night long, all I heard was 'dat dat dat dat dat' with the goddamn elevator cable banging into the wall when it moved up and down," he said.

He even went to the front desk to ask for a new room, but they were sold out.

It may sound funny coming from me, but sometimes purely playing the heel just doesn't pay off. It's better to play the good guy. It was easy to learn just from watching how others acted and reacted. I would learn how to handle things and how not to handle things, using my "Inner Brain" for good and not evil.

While Baron Leone loved to rile up a crowd, he also knew when to play the good guy and entertain people in situations where he could have easily been the heel. A lot of wrestlers would get speeding tickets from cops. Most of them would just say, "Okay, Barney. Just give me the ticket and I'll go," playing the bad guy who got caught with his hand in the cookie jar. Not Leone. He would speed down the road with his pants open, not exposing himself, but similar to what you would do if you were sitting in front of the television after a big meal. He would also wear a hat and chew on a cigar.

Eventually, the cop would catch up to him and pull him over. He would ask Leone to get out of the car. He would get out and stand up, which made his pants fall to the ground. He would bend over to pull them up and his hat would fall off. He would reach down to get his hat and the cigar would fall out of his mouth. The cop would be laughing so hard that he would just let him go. Essentially, Leone used his "Inner Brain" to entertain and play the funny good guy and the heel who wanted to get out of the ticket at the same time. More often than not, he would get away with it.

He broke the law by speeding, but he also gave the cops a good laugh when they probably needed it, not to mention a story to tell his buddies. He didn't complain or insult the officer like we both saw others do. When you work in front of large groups of many different types of people, you and your "Inner Brain" learn what works and what doesn't work. Leone knew that if he could entertain the cops, they would hopefully forget about his speeding. He may have gotten a ticket after all, but he just allowed his funny side to come through, as opposed to playing the heel.

Being a babyface for cops almost always works, especially when they know who you are and they are wrestling fans. Gene Okerlund and I were at the NATPE convention in San Francisco many years ago to promote a wrestling program. There would be these huge parties with the biggest at the Billy Graham Pavilion, named after an old rock-and-roll promoter. They had the Ronettes, Frankie Valli, and Sha Na Na playing there and it was just an opportunity to schmooze. The tickets were free but hard to come by. I even had to hit up Geraldo Rivera, whom I've know for a long time, to see if he had any tickets. No luck. Maybe he should have looked in Al Capone's vault.

After trying my best, I told Okerlund that there weren't any tickets, but that wasn't the end of it. My "Inner Brain" would not allow me to just walk away. I had to do this. We had dinner at a nearby restaurant when this cop walked in and started talking to the maitre d'. We found out that he wanted to meet us and get our autographs. I was about to sign something for him when I had an idea cooking in my "Inner Brain." I told him that I had some 8x10 pictures that I could sign for him if he did me a favor.

He drove us in his squad car back to the concert at the Pavilion. Right in front of the guy taking tickets at the entrance, the cop pulled us out with both our hands behind our backs and yelled, "Now get in there. If I catch you guys back here one more time, I'll throw you in jail."

We didn't need a ticket after all and the cop got his autographed 8x10. We did him a favor, and he did us a favor.

But playing the good guy in certain situations also means that you act grateful and unselfish toward others who really come through for you with kindness, not concert tickets or free drinks. "Bobby the Brain" would never do that, but I've been fortunate to meet people who have shown me that kindness, and I have been more fortunate to return those favors. I would like to think it's a part of my "Inner Brain."

Northwest Airlines used to have a private room at the airports for people who were frequent fliers, but you had to join and there was a fee associated with the membership. It was very convenient and you could even drink for free, which was always a bonus. I had regular flights that flew out of Chicago. At this one private room, there was this Japanese woman named Miako who was very nice. One night, my flight was delayed and Miako felt a little sorry for me and let me wait in the room even though I wasn't a member. I was exhausted, sat myself down on a chair, and fell asleep. This sweet woman closed up and let me sleep there all night. In the morning, another woman unlocked the door, walked in, and woke me up, asking me what I was doing there. I told her that Miako let me sleep here.

From that point on, every time I was in Chicago, I would buy Miako one rose and she would treat me like a member of the "club." I'd drink six to seven beers and even bring my friends in. She treated me like a king, not a heel.

The lesson here is that I could have bitched about the plane being delayed, but I decided to use my "Inner Brain" to be the nice guy and Miako paid me back with her thoughtfulness. That's a good lesson in life. Playing the babyface side of your "Inner Brain" may not always pay off, but at least you can say you tried.

And hopefully you don't have to pretend to be your own "twin brother."

I've been a heel in the ring, but sometimes fans wouldn't catch what I was doing, because it would have nothing to do with what was supposed to be going on during the match. I wasn't as demonstrative as I was at ringside. I was just being mischievous and using my "Inner Brain." Ray Stevens and I were wrestling one Halloween night many years ago. Before the match, we put shoe polish on our fingertips. When we were in the ring, we'd do the old raking of the fingernails on a guy's back. Our opponent would sell it, but he would end up with stripes on his back like a tiger.

Greg Gagne saw what was going on and walked to ringside during the match. He yelled at us, "You're going to kill this town!" I looked at this crowd that would never show up to another AWA show again. I counted nine. He was pissing me off and got just close enough to me so I could stick him in the eye with my thumb just to get him away from me—paint and all.

When I wrestled Greg, my "Inner Brain" would have fun in the ring with him. I would always put him in a full nelson and then bang his head into the turnbuckle. But Greg never knew how to take that move. When he tried to do it, he'd end up behind me. One night, I tried to do it again, but this time I heard an awful noise. I looked at him and his broken nose with blood all over his face from the back of my head.

Another night in Peoria, I threw him outside the ring, and he was lying on the floor. Some fan had a chair in his hand and was ready to throw it in the ring. He tossed it, and I watched it go over my head and land on Greg's face, breaking his nose all over again. He broke his nose twice in the same month with me.

I told him, "It could have been worse. It could have been me."

Seriously, Greg was a great worker. He had a heck of a match with Nick Bockwinkel one night in Sioux City, Iowa. As a rule, I never jumped up during a babyface comeback or when a heel was getting heat. I would just act concerned and throw my little tantrum at ringside.

That night, out of "frustration," I kicked this chair, and it took a funny kind of bounce. I heard the people react and the light bulb went on and my "Inner Brain" went to work. So, I kicked it again, but this time I got my foot caught in it. Then I kicked it into the ring post and it bounced back and hit me. I dropped an elbow on it. I even threw it on top of me as if it was going to pin me. There I was, having a match with a chair. Meanwhile, Gagne and Bockwinkel are in this prolonged rest hold just so they could watch everything. It was just another example of how I and my "Inner Brain" love to entertain and have fun in life.

I'm international in my entertaining. My "Inner Brain" transcends all cultures.

One time, as I was going through customs in Canada, the guy behind the counter asked me, "Where are you from?"

I said, "The United States."

"Do you have any proof?"

"I have deodorant," I said.

"Go ahead," he said and let me go.

In Japan, wrestling fans would walk into the building, take their shoes off, and put them in these pigeon holes, sort of like mailboxes. They would put on slippers and sit on the floor. I don't know why. It was just a cultural thing. I had nothing to do one day and when I was bored and then came the mischievous side of the "Inner Brain" in me. I worked the last match one night and on a Japanese card, they would feature six Japanese matches and six matches where it was Americans vs. the Japanese. If fans would go for a month straight, they would see the same match every night. There was really nothing to do before or after my match.

I decided to go to the front of the building. I saw all the shoes neatly arranged in these mailboxes. I couldn't have that, so I switched all the shoes. After the matches were over, I just sat back and watched them to see what would happen. Then, it hit me. All the shoes were pretty much the same size, which was small. It didn't work. The "Inner Brain" was foiled.

At Buckingham Palace, there are always about a couple hundred people taking pictures outside the complex. There's a big flagpole in view and if the flag is up, the Queen is home. If the flag is down, she's away.

My wife and I were standing in front of the palace when the gates started to open. That gave me an idea and brought out my "Inner Brain." My philosophy about a lot of things is what is the penalty for the crime? If I moon somebody as a 16-year-old kid, I'm not going to death row or have a guy named Bubba in my cell at night. I would get my hand slapped and just get a scare put on me. I'd ask the jury if any one of them has mooned or been mooned. Then I'd form a cult called the "White Ovals."

So, I was thinking to myself, "What would be the penalty if I did what I wanted to do?" I walked through the gates and toward the palace. The guards stopped me, "I'm sorry, sir, you can't see her."

I said, "Excuse me, I just want to ask you a question. How far is Buckingham Palace Square?" (Keep in mind I knew where it was.)

"It's right up the street there, sir."

"How long will it take for me to walk there?"

"About 20 minutes," the guard said.

"Thank you. I'm so sorry to bother you," I said.

"No, that's all right."

"Thank you," I said as I walked away.

I get back to where all the people are and turned around, yelling to the guard, "How long did you say?"

He yelled back, "Twenty minutes."

I said to my wife for everyone else to hear, "He told me that the Queen is coming out in 20 minutes to sign autographs."

Everyone around me started loading their cameras like mad, including my wife. I had to pull her away, and she started whining. I told her the truth, "Do you think the Queen is coming out and see this bunch of ham-and-eggers hang on her fence and sign autographs?"

I had 200 to 250 people buying into it. I don't know how long they even waited.

Unleashing your "Inner Brain" can be done in any situation and if you're in any physical condition. They say patience is a virtue. Well, if the patient are virtuous, then I'm a whore, kind of like Trixie. I hate lines, whether it is for flying, getting a rental car, or waiting for a hotel room. Even if you're facing a long line of people—or humanoids—you can use real-life situations or afflictions to your advantage.

I was in New York to do a signing of the first book. I checked into my hotel the day after a major snowstorm that practically closed the entire city. Do I have good timing or what? Everything was open, but there was no way to get anywhere. In front of me, there was a long line to the check-in desk and the lobby was full of people on top of that.

I had just had a cyst removed from my hip. While the pain had subsided somewhat since my surgery, it was still there. But even if I wanted to get some immediate help, everyone working there was buried in work or busy with a customer. I was determined not to stand in line and I knew there had to be another way around it.

I let that "Inner Brain" out.

I limped up to the back of the line, rather exaggeratedly. No one noticed. So, I dropped my bag a couple of times to see if I could get anyone's attention. No one noticed. Some "Inner Brain" I have. I added a few "oh shits" to the bag dropping. Finally, someone from the hotel walked up to me. "Are you okay, sir?" they asked.

I said, "I'm fine. I'll make it. I need no help. I ask for nothing."

I had them all in the palm of my hand.

He led me to the concierge past all the people and right to the front of the line, "Excuse me ma'am," I said, stumbling over the plant and everything in sight just for added effect. "I'm supposed to check in here today and as you can see I've had open-hip surgery on my thurm."

I have absolutely no idea what or where a thurm is.

"I can't really stand in line to check in," I continued. "My thurm is aggravated, and I have to get myself upstairs somehow and ice this or it swells. I wouldn't be able to walk if that happened. I'd be here for a month and would probably have to be taken to the emergency room. I have an antibiotic, Neutrali (my "Inner Brain" made that up, too) that I have to take as well very soon."

"Just a minute," she said.

Hook, line, and sinker.

She went to the front desk and came back with my key and everything.

"Can someone help you up with your bag?" she asked.

"That would be awful nice of you." Keep in mind, I had a bag with wheels, but they were willing to roll it for me.

Again, adding a little drama, I said to the bellhop, "Would you mind if I hold on to your shoulder?"

"Not at all," he said.

We get off the elevator. I said, "I think I can take it from here."

"Are you sure you're all right?" he asked.

I paused, slapped my hip/"thurm" twice and said, "Good as new." I walked away as if nothing was wrong with me.

I got that idea from the time Nick Bockwinkel and I were at an airport to fly from Atlanta to Minneapolis on a 747 that was going to be packed with probably about 300 people. They were all in line. I met Nick at the terminal, and he shrugged his shoulders and gave me a look like, "What can we do?"

I knew what to do. The "Inner Brain" went immediately to work.

I walked up to the counter, limping all the way past the people, and got the attention of the guy behind the counter. "Sir, I just had knee surgery and I can't stand in this line."

"Give me that," he said with a smile. He took my ticket and stamped it. I walked around the corner out of view from him but still in full view of the people who were still waiting in the line. I slapped my knee twice and said, "Good as new." No longer limping, I walked right onto the plane.

Nick found me on the plane after waiting in that long line, "You know, everyone turned their heads and watched you when you slapped your knee."

I smiled.

"How's your leg now?" he asked.

"Good as new."

He didn't find that particularly funny.

"You're just mad because you're not as smart as me," I said. "You had to stand in line and you're in coach. I'm in first class."

"By the way, Nick, when you leave, make sure you pull the curtain."

Then I ordered another scotch and water.

I didn't really hurt anybody in either of those situations. They all would have boarded the plane anyway and gotten to their assigned seats. Yes, I lied about my leg, hip, and "thurm," but I didn't want to stand, and one time, I was probably not healthy enough to be on my feet for that long. Besides, by the time I would have gotten on the plane, it would have been crowded and I wouldn't have been able to put my bag in the overhead. Okay, that's no excuse. I was just a little smarter than those people, including Nick Bockwinkel, not to mention the hotel and the airline.

I stole nothing. I didn't take anything someone else would have had. Like kids say, I butted in line. I used my "Inner Brain" to save a little time. No harm. No foul. Just good, clean fun.

Unleashing my "Inner Brain" has not slowed down, even if I have. Sometimes, the smallest tasks will bring out that kid who planted his pencil box or ordered pizzas for the neighbor. Sometimes, opportunity knocks for the "Inner Brain," and I just have to answer that door.

My wife was involved with a bake sale for the church that we attend. She put something together and put a sticker on the wrapper with her name on it. She asked me to run it over to the church and set it in the church's gym for her.

What could she have been thinking?

I took it over to the church and found the gym. Inside, there had to be more than 100 cakes, pies, donuts, and any other type of baked good you can imagine. And everyone made sure that their names were attached to the items they made.

It was time to go to work.

Mind you, it took me an hour, but I switched everybody's sticker, label, or card. I managed to reassign every baked item in there, including Cindi's of course.

After the sale was over, everybody would compliment Cindi on the great carrot cake she made.

The only problem was she made muffins.

Again, no harm done. The church raised some money, I had some fun, and my wife now has the reputation for making the best carrot cake in our church. People at our church are still asking for the recipe.

The "Inner Brain" strikes again.

CHAPTER 18

WWTBDAS?
(What Would "The Brain" Do and Say?)

I think I'm the perfect person to write a self-help book. Because I know what parasites and losers that relatives and neighbors can be. Even your own wife and kids, they want to mooch off you. Everyone has guilt except me. I'm kind of like Jim Jones without Kool-Aid. I'd like to help you people because I've been all over the world and I've seen every type of lowlife imaginable. I've done my best to try to help people out. Right now, I'm helping out an orphanage in Guam, but I don't want to get into that right now. Modesty forbids me from doing it, but an address in Beverly Hills for donations will be listed later. Make sure you send cash.

A lot of people don't even help themselves. They help other people. They bend over backwards. I see it more as they're bending over forward and taking it from people.

My advice to you humanoids is to immediately make friends with your neighbors. Do the best you can to share your life with them. Open up to them. After all, communication is the key in life. But be specific and spare no detail. Explain how your back is bad, so maybe they can mow your grass for you or their punk kid could do it instead of breaking somebody's windows, the little bastard. The same goes for your relatives. You can explain to your

"You can lead a gift horse to water, but that doesn't mean it's a duck."

in-laws that you'd love to have them over for the Christmas holidays, but the back room caught on fire when Aunt Edna came by and her respirator short-circuited.

And make sure you don't make them feel bad about sending the gifts. Accept them and let them know how much trouble they must have gone through when they shopped for you and how you don't want to see them standing in long lines to return the presents.

It's funny in a way. I'm writing a self-help book when I portrayed a person who would consider self-help to be "help thyself." Imagine "The Brain" writing a self-help book and having his say.

"It's about time. My voice needs to be heard and all you humanoids will benefit from what I'm writing. I do live by the adage, 'Help thyself.' I'm not going to help anyone out, unless it's out of their wallet.

"I am the man to go to for advice. Some people give you good advice and some people give you bad advice. Mine is golden and will get you through the challenges in life. And I have no ulterior motives. Just ask any man I managed. Some people would say that I'm a dime a dozen and there are a lot out there like me. Well, if there are, they're ripping me off and need to start paying me royalties. Take their advice with a grain of salt. Take mine after you give me a big pile of money. Consider the source. Consider 'The Brain' for advice when you're facing adversity.

"I am the kind of guy who makes friends easily. I'll make friends with anyone who has the nerve to block my way. I'll gain their confidence, which is a good idea. It is easy to find out what their fears are and then you can easily topple him. Consider this option. Date the humanoid's daughter just to drive him nuts or if he happens to have a buck or two in the bank.

"I'm also qualified to give out advice to all you ham-and-eggers because I am a well-educated individual. Unfortunately, the school I went to burned to the ground many years ago and all the records were destroyed. Modesty prevents me from keeping any diplomas and awards. I was at that school every day in my Rolls Royce. I know, you think that means I never actually walked into the school. Well, I'll thank you all to mind your own business. I went to the finest schools, from elementary on up, and I was a model student, both in and out of the classroom. Sometimes, when a girl would mysteriously get her pigtails dipped in the inkwell, I was always there to help. I would recommend a good place to get it washed out. So what if my brother-in-law owned the place?

"After school, I became the best manager in professional wrestling. I considered my 'Bobby Heenan family' to be a true team effort. Not that I was a member of the team, but my men were unified. They didn't need to know what I was doing to—I mean for—them. Andre the Giant was a great meal ticket for me, and I would never say anything bad about him—to his face. He was difficult to manage. He would never take my advice in the ring and out of the ring, including that fertilizer farm that I invested in on his behalf. Things happen.

"Nick Bockwinkel was a well-versed and educated man and some people accused me of riding on his coattails. I had my fair share of intelligence too, and Nick benefited from my wisdom. He became a smarter man under my guidance. He was a champion and was a good source of income as well. Business is business.

"Haku and the Islanders had problems deciding on what to have for lunch, and that's why they needed me. I admit that I took a larger percentage from them, but it's not like they needed Mercedes cars and big houses in Beverly Hills. A lean-to in a city park would suffice, and they could stay there for days. If they're hungry, there are plenty of trash containers around. There are birds and sunshine. What more do they need? It's just like home in Samoa. They were more than happy.

"The money they did earn was invested well. Banks are not my style. I found this great nudie bar in Sweden. I'm not sure whatever happened to them and I've never gone into one of those sleazy places. But from what I've heard, you can make a little money by putting a dollar in her g-string and pull two out. If you get caught, just tell the broad that the dollars were slipping and you were just trying to save them for her.

"The goal is to stay one step ahead of your enemies and your friends because you never know when an ally is going to become your foe. Many wrestling fans think that I always got it in the end when someone I was managing turned on me, but what they don't know is that I was usually planning on dumping the bum anyway.

"Having that 'family' makes me an expert on running a family. If I had a daughter, I'd spoil her. If I had a wife I would let her know immediately who was in charge from the beginning. If she didn't like it, she could hit the bricks. But I wouldn't make her a prisoner. We could host neighborhood parties as long as she did all the work. Well, not all the work. I would be in charge of coats and make sure that the coat pockets were well protected.

"Divorce would not be an option for her, and I would only do it if she paid for it. Now, if a friend was going through a divorce, I would suggest to him a good Beverly Hills lawyer. While he may be occupied for the next six months to a year, I would have my friend sign over the power of attorney to me so his wife doesn't get it. He would have nothing to worry about and there would be no pressure. After all, I already live in a home.

"But I would want to cover all my bases and make sure that I'm not taking sides. You never want to do that. I'd go to my friend's wife and say, 'Your husband just approached me and he wants to give me power of attorney. I really don't want to get involved in it. I never really cared for the guy. I think you're getting a bum deal. To cover yourself, sweetheart, you give me power of attorney. I don't think you can have power of attorney for two people at the same time, so I can tell him that I have power of attorney from say my sister-in-law. He won't bug me about it and, more importantly, he won't know that I have your power of attorney.'

"I would have both powers of attorney, and it wouldn't be my fault if they were bankrupted and living in a soup kitchen. And if there was a sign in front of each house that said, 'House for Sale by Owner,' it would only be to try to save the friendship and get material things out of the way. After all, I have an orphanage to fund.

"Divorce can be ugly and my ideas are to help make the best of things. If there are children involved, that can get expensive with alimony and child support. My suggestion is to switch the DNA with your brother and then claim to be sterile, gay, or mysteriously drugged with your sperm being extracted from your body, maybe by a group of aliens.

"The best advice to give anyone thinking about getting married is to never marry a midget wrestler. The only reason you would do that is if you don't want to do a lot of ironing.

"As far as an extended family, we'd always be at Thanksgiving dinner. That's where I would teach everyone about sacrifice. Take the drumsticks on the turkey for example. Many people don't know that dark meat is high in fat and salt, so I'd insist on taking both, since I have a stronger constitution. After dinner, I'd make sure that cigars would be passed around so we could all relax and talk. Sometimes, the cigars I pass out are bigger than the bands around it. Yes, I put the bands on, but they fell off when the cigars got too dry. I can't afford a nice humidor because of that orphanage I'm supporting.

"While I'm a role model, others have been role models in my life. Presidents like Richard Nixon and Bill Clinton are fine examples on how to live your life. I don't judge people based on their political views, but how they conduct their lives. Remember, Nixon told the truth when he said that famous line, 'I am not a crook.' Did I tell you that I was a secret advisor to him and told him to say that line? I should have gotten some money for that. And while I'm thinking about it, I am selling Monica's dress on Ebay, along with Mark McGuire's 70th home run ball. But hurry up. I'm down to my last eight of each. Of course, the money goes to the orphanage.

"On the business end, every executive at Enron is a true example of how to run a business. Never refuse a bribe. That would be rude. In thinking about it, I think those guys stole a few ideas from me when I ran my 'family.'

"Those honorable men taught us that laws don't apply to everyone, just the suckers who abide by them. If you get pulled over for speeding, there's no need to get a ticket. Here's what you do. When Barney Fife asks for your driver's license, put a bill right under the license, but make sure he can see that picture of George Washington. If he asks you, 'Are you offering me a bribe?' you have an immediate answer.

"'Do you really think I'd bribe you with a dollar? It got stuck to my hand from the medicine I had to use on my skin after pulling kids out of a burning school bus on the way to the police athletic league to donate money.'

"You need to be frugal with your money. Financial responsibility is the key. Eating at restaurants is a nice luxury, but can get expensive. So, you have to use cost-cutting methods. If someone at the next table left a huge tip, it may be too much for just one waitress. So take part of that tip or even all of it so you can look like a big tipper and take care of your waitress, who worked a little harder. But if the meal is too pricey, keep a cockroach with you at all times and put in on the plate when you're done with dinner.

"Blind guys playing the saxophone are a nice source of income, too. They don't need all that change and, besides, they don't miss it. Hell, get yourself a pair of sunglasses and a sax and play for the people. Entertain them and pick up some spare change along the way. I know that they rarely get paper money, but that's because most people are cheapskates.

"Another great source of income is to own a funeral home. The Bobby Heenan Funeral Home would provide services beyond just dealing with dead people. We would be more than happy to sell the shoes, rings, watches, wigs, glasses, and even the gold out of their teeth so the bereaved don't have to be burdened with it or reminded of their loved ones.

"You can pick up a nice suit from it and if someone asks you why the back isn't sewn up, tell him that you got it from a ventriloquist. And if they smell formaldehyde, tell them it's some English Leather gone bad.

"Look, if someone does approach you with problems and there isn't any financial gain that you can see, tell them, 'Stand on your own two feet. Be a man. In fact, be like Bobby Heenan. You don't see him sniveling and crying, do you?'

"That's the only way to do it. Tell them to suck it up and deal with it. You have to go forth. You have to go headfirst into battle. There are no two ways about it. Grin and bear it. Keep a stiff upper lip. Then, pat him on the back and go through his pocket as you're walking him out the door.

"Money is the key. It is the only thing that will help you and solve your problems. So, if everyone gives me all their money, I will tell you how you can help the most important person you can help. Me. If it doesn't make sense to you, don't worry about it. It makes sense to me. So, if you're thumbing through this book at the bookstore or Wal-mart because you're cheap, my advice is to buy this book, you deadbeat.

"To sum up, self-help is exactly what it means. Backwards, it means 'help me.' Help Bobby 'The Brain' Heenan."

The best way to describe the Bobby Heenan character is a joke I've often heard.

Heenan and his friends, Tom and Bill, are standing in front of a casket of a longtime buddy. Tom says to his friend, "You know, I'm sorry you died. Here's that 50 bucks I owe you from the Super Bowl."

Bill then says, "I didn't pay you either for that Super Bowl bet. Here's the $100 I bet you on."

"The Brain" would say, "I bet $200 with you, but I don't have the change."

So he writes him a check for $350, puts it in his friend's pocket and takes the $150 out.

Stay away from the Bobby Heenans of the world. Believe nothing that they say. Besides, anyone who bleaches his hair, wears neon suits, and has a nickname like "Pretty Boy" and "The Brain" should be avoided at all costs. Does he look honest? Not really. He talks too fast and says nothing. Who knows if he ever had cancer to being with? He could be working the slurred speech gimmick.

Bobby Heenans have no conscience. Don't expect them to be part of the big scams, but the little ones, because they simply don't know how to make the big score. He can't even con people properly because he's not all that smart. He'd never try to scam his way into Major League Baseball. The minor leagues would be just fine with him. If he got hold of an old woman's charge card, he wouldn't take thousands of dollars. He'd use it to buy a cheap, mismatched suit or buy everyone a drink at his favorite waffle house.

Don't be a "Bobby Heenan." I'm not even saying to be a Ray Heenan. Just be a clown. That's the best advice I can give anyone.

Well, that's about it. Now when do I get paid?

Celebrate the Heroes of American Sports
in These Other 2004 Releases from Sports Publishing!

Matt Kenseth:
Above and Beyond
by Kelley Maruszewski
(Kenseth's sister)

• 10 x 10 hardcover • 160 pages
• color photos throughout
• $24.95

Jack Arute's Tales
from the Indy 500
by Jack Arute and Jenna Fryer

• 5.5 x 8.25 hardcover
• 200 pages • photos throughout
• $19.95

Fred Claire: My 30
Years in Dodger Blue
by Fred Claire with Steve
Springer

• 6 x 9 hardcover • 200 pages
• photos throughout
• $24.95

Mark Martin:
Mark of Excellence
by Larry Woody

• 10 x 10 hardcover • 160 pages
• color photos throughout
• $24.95

Good as Gold: Techniques
for Fundamental Baseball
by Frank White
with Matt Fulks

• 7 x 10 softcover
• 224 pages
• photos throughout
• $19.95

Ryan Newman:
Engineer for Speed
by Deb Williams

• 6 x 9 hardcover • 210 pages
• photos throughout
• $24.95

Larry Bowa:
I Still Hate to Lose
by Larry Bowa
with Barry M. Bloom

• 6 x 9 hardcover • 250 pages
• photos throughout
• $24.95

Kenny Bernstein:
King of Speed
by Kenny Bernstein
with Bill Stephens

• 10 x 10 hardcover • 160 pages
• color photos throughout
• $24.95

The Memoirs of Bing Devine:
Stealing Lou Brock and
Other Brilliant Moves by a
Master G.M.
by Bing Devine
with Tom Wheatley

• 6 x 9 hardcover • 225 pages
• photos throughout • $24.95

Tales from the Drag
Strip with "Big Daddy" Don
Garlits
by Don Garlits with Bill
Stephens

• 5.5 x 8.25 hardcover
• 200 pages • photos throughout
• $19.95